KYOTO TRAVEL GUIDE 2023 AND BEYOND

Unveiling Kyoto's Timeless Beauty Temples, Zen Gardens, and Traditional Japanese Arts

By: Haru Hinata

CONTENTS

INTRODUCTION

Welcome to Kyoto, a city that embodies the rich cultural heritage and timeless beauty of Japan. Nestled amidst the picturesque landscapes of the Kansai region, Kyoto is a treasure trove of ancient temples, serene Zen gardens, and traditional Japanese arts. Steeped in history and tradition, this city seamlessly blends the past with the present, offering visitors a glimpse into Japan's captivating heritage.

As you embark on your journey through Kyoto, prepare to be enchanted by its awe-inspiring temples, meticulously designed gardens, and the profound tranquility that permeates its atmosphere. Whether you are seeking spiritual enlightenment, a deeper connection with nature, or simply a moment of respite from the bustling modern world, Kyoto has something to offer every visitor.

Throughout this travel guide, we will explore some of Kyoto's most revered temples, unveil the secrets of its Zen gardens, and delve into the world of traditional Japanese arts. From the iconic Kinkaku-ji Temple, also known as the Golden Pavilion, to the serene beauty of Ryoan-ji's rock garden, Kyoto's cultural treasures are sure to leave an indelible impression on your heart and mind.

KYOTO ORIGIN AND HISTORY

The city of Kyoto, located in the Kansai region of Japan, has a rich and fascinating origin and history. Here's an overview of its origin and historical development:

Origin of Kyoto

Kyoto, originally known as Heian-kyo, was established as the capital of Japan in 794 CE by Emperor Kammu. The decision to move the capital from Nara to Heian-kyo was driven by political and cultural reasons. The new capital was strategically located in a central area of Japan and had a more defensible position against potential invasions.

History of Kyoto

Heian Period (794-1185)

During the Heian period, Kyoto became the center of Japanese culture, art, and literature. It was an era of relative peace and stability, and the imperial court thrived as the aristocracy developed a refined and elegant culture. Many influential works of Japanese literature, such as "The Tale of Genji" by Murasaki Shikibu, were written during this period.

Medieval Period (1185-1603)

In the late 12th century, political power shifted from the imperial court to the samurai class, leading to a period of feudalism known as the Kamakura and Muromachi periods. Kyoto remained an important cultural and religious center during this time. Zen Buddhism flourished, and many temples and Zen gardens were established, leaving a lasting impact on the city's landscape.

Azuchi-Momoyama Period (1568-1603)

During this period, Japan experienced a brief unification under powerful warlords, notably Oda Nobunaga and Toyotomi Hideyoshi. Kyoto saw a period of cultural and artistic revival. Notable architectural achievements, such as Nijo Castle, were constructed, showcasing the power and grandeur of the ruling elite.

Edo Period (1603-1868)

In 1603, the Tokugawa shogunate established its government in Edo (present-day Tokyo), bringing about a long period of peace and stability. Kyoto, although no longer the political capital, remained an important cultural and religious center. The imperial court retained its influence, and the city continued to thrive as a hub for traditional arts, crafts, and the practice of tea ceremonies.

Modern Era (1868-present)

With the Meiji Restoration in 1868, the imperial capital was officially moved to Tokyo. Kyoto's role shifted to becoming a center for preserving and showcasing Japan's rich cultural heritage. The city's historic temples, shrines, and traditional arts attracted scholars, artists, and tourists from around the world.

2023 and Beyond

Today, Kyoto stands as a living testament to Japan's rich history and traditions. Its well-preserved temples, historic districts, and traditional arts continue to draw visitors who seek to immerse themselves in the timeless beauty and cultural heritage of the city.

Seasonal Beauty

Kyoto is a city that offers distinct beauty in each season. Here's a glimpse of the seasonal beauty you can experience in Kyoto:

Spring (March to May)

Spring in Kyoto is a magical time, especially during cherry blossom season (late March to early April). Visit parks and temples such as Maruyama Park, Philosopher's Path, and the grounds of Kiyomizu-dera to witness the ethereal beauty of cherry blossoms in full bloom. The delicate pink petals create a stunning backdrop for traditional architecture and provide a sense of tranquility throughout the city.

Summer (June to August)

While summers in Kyoto can be hot and humid, there are still some captivating experiences to enjoy. Take a stroll along the Kamo River and enjoy the cool breeze. Explore the lush gardens of temples such as Nanzen-ji and Tofuku-ji, which offer shade and respite from the heat. You can also visit the Gion Matsuri festival in July, one of Japan's most famous festivals featuring colorful processions and traditional performances.

Autumn (September to November)

Autumn is another spectacular season in Kyoto when the city is transformed by vibrant foliage. The maple trees create a fiery tapestry of red, orange, and gold hues. Iconic spots to visit during this time include Arashiyama's bamboo forest, Eikando Temple, and the gardens of Kiyomizu-dera. Take a stroll through the Philosopher's Path or visit the mountainous areas such as Kurama or Takao for breathtaking autumn scenery.

Winter (December to February)

Winter in Kyoto offers a serene and quieter atmosphere. The city is adorned with festive illuminations, especially in Arashiyama and along the streets of Higashiyama. You can visit temples and shrines such as Kinkaku-ji and Fushimi Inari Taisha with fewer crowds. Additionally, soaking in an outdoor hot spring (onsen) in nearby areas like Kurama or Arashiyama can be a rejuvenating experience during the colder months.

TRAVEL PRACTICALITIES

Traveling to Kyoto can be an enriching and memorable experience. To make your trip smooth and enjoyable, here are some practicalities and travel tips to keep in mind:

Visa Requirements

Japan has specific visa requirements based on the nationality of the traveler and the purpose of their visit. Here are some general guidelines:

Visa Exemption

Citizens of many countries are allowed to enter Japan without a visa for short-term stays for tourism, business, or transit purposes. The visa exemption duration varies depending on the country, but it typically ranges from 15 to 90 days. Travelers must have a valid passport and meet certain conditions, such as having a return or onward ticket.

Visa on Arrival

Japan offers visa on arrival to some nationalities for short stays. However, this option is generally available for travelers from countries that don't have Japanese diplomatic missions.

Visa Application

For travelers who need a visa to enter Japan, they must apply for the appropriate visa at a Japanese embassy or consulate in their home country. The application process may require submitting various documents, such as passport, visa application form, photo, flight itinerary, hotel reservation, proof of sufficient funds, and a detailed itinerary of the trip.

Types of Visas

Japan offers various types of visas for different purposes, including tourist visa, business visa, student visa, working visa, and more. The requirements and processing time for each type of visa may vary, so it's essential to check the specific requirements for the intended purpose of your visit.

Validity and Extensions

Visa validity and allowed stay duration depend on the type of visa granted. Some visas may be valid for single or multiple entries, and the permitted stay duration may vary. If you wish to extend your stay beyond the visa's validity, you need to apply for an extension at the local immigration office in Japan before your current visa expires.

Changes and Updates

Visa requirements and regulations can change, and it's essential to verify the latest information and updates from the official website of the Japanese embassy or consulate in your country before making travel arrangements.

Best Time to Visit

The best time to visit Kyoto depends on your preferences for weather, activities, and the type of experience you seek. Kyoto experiences distinct seasons, each offering its own unique charm. Here's a breakdown of the different seasons:

Spring (March to May)

Spring is one of the most popular times to visit Kyoto. The city comes alive with cherry blossoms (sakura) in late March to early April, creating a breathtaking spectacle of pink flowers. The weather is generally mild and pleasant, making it ideal for outdoor activities and sightseeing. However, this is also the busiest tourist season, so expect larger crowds and higher accommodation prices. Be sure to book well in advance if planning a spring visit.

Autumn (September to November)

Autumn is another peak season for tourists in Kyoto. The city's landscapes transform into a colorful palette of red, orange, and yellow hues as the leaves change during the fall foliage season. The weather remains comfortable, and there are numerous autumn festivals and events to enjoy. As with spring, it's essential to book accommodations in advance during this popular season.

Summer (June to August)

Summer in Kyoto can be hot and humid, with temperatures often exceeding 30°C (86°F). While the weather can be challenging, this season offers various summer festivals and events, such as Gion Matsuri in July. Additionally, if you don't mind the heat, you can take advantage of fewer crowds and potentially lower accommodation rates.

Winter (December to February)

Winter in Kyoto is relatively mild compared to other regions of Japan, but temperatures can still drop, especially in January and February. While it's the low tourist season, you can experience a quieter and more peaceful atmosphere in the city. Some attractions may have shorter operating hours, but you can enjoy Kyoto's winter illuminations and traditional New Year's celebrations.

Getting to Kyoto

Kyoto is a well-connected city with several transportation options to reach it from major cities within Japan and international destinations. Here are the common ways to get to Kyoto:

By Air

The nearest major international airport to Kyoto is Kansai International Airport (KIX), located approximately 100 kilometers (62 miles) southwest of Kyoto. KIX serves as the primary gateway to Kyoto for international travelers. From the airport, you can reach Kyoto by various means, including:

Train

Take the Haruka Express train from KIX to Kyoto Station. The journey takes around 75-90 minutes, and the train offers comfortable and efficient transportation.

Airport Limousine Bus

Airport limousine buses also operate between KIX and Kyoto Station. The journey time is approximately 90-120 minutes, depending on traffic.

Transportation within Kyoto

Transportation within Kyoto is efficient and well-developed, making it easy for visitors to explore the city and its many attractions. Here are the main modes of transportation within Kyoto:

Bus

Kyoto has an extensive bus network that covers most areas of the city, including popular tourist destinations. City buses are an excellent way to get around and are often the most convenient option for visiting temples, shrines, and other historical sites. Bus routes are well-marked in English, and electronic displays announce upcoming stops and provide information in multiple languages. You can pay the fare in cash when boarding the bus, or use an IC card like Suica or ICOCA for cashless payment.

Subway

Kyoto has two subway lines, the Karasuma Line and the Tozai Line, which connect major areas of the city. The subway is fast and efficient, particularly for longer distances. The subway stations are conveniently located near popular attractions and shopping districts.

Trains

In addition to the subway, Kyoto also has JR (Japan Railways) lines, including the JR Sagano Line and the JR Nara Line.

These JR lines are useful for getting to certain destinations, such as Arashiyama and Fushimi Inari Taisha.

Kyoto City Bus & Subway Pass

If you plan to use public transportation extensively, consider purchasing the Kyoto City Bus & Subway Pass. This pass allows unlimited rides on Kyoto buses and subways for a specified duration (1 day, 2 days, or 3 days), offering good value for money.

Taxi

Taxis are readily available in Kyoto and can be hailed on the street or found at taxi stands near major transportation hubs and tourist attractions. Taxis are convenient for short trips or when traveling in a group. Note that taxis can be more expensive compared to buses and subways.

Bicycle Rental

Renting a bicycle is a popular and enjoyable way to explore Kyoto, especially in areas with bike-friendly lanes and paths. Many rental shops offer bicycles for daily or hourly use, and cycling allows you to experience the city at a leisurely pace.

Walking

Kyoto's city center is relatively compact, and many of its iconic attractions are within walking distance of each other. Walking is a pleasant way to discover hidden gems and immerse yourself in Kyoto's unique ambiance.

Accommodation

Kyoto offers a wide range of accommodation options to suit various preferences and budgets. From traditional ryokans (Japanese inns) to modern hotels, you can find a place to stay that enhances your experience in this historical city. Here are some popular accommodation choices in Kyoto:

Ryokans

Ryokans are traditional Japanese inns that provide an authentic cultural experience. They typically feature tatami-matted rooms, futon bedding, and traditional kaiseki meals. Staying in a ryokan allows you to immerse yourself in Japanese hospitality and customs. Some ryokans are located near famous temples or in scenic areas, offering a serene and relaxing atmosphere.

Hotels

Kyoto has a wide selection of hotels, ranging from budget-friendly options to luxury accommodations. You can find Western-style hotels with modern amenities, as well as boutique hotels that blend traditional and contemporary design. Hotels in Kyoto often offer a mix of Japanese hospitality and international service standards.

Guesthouses and Hostels

For budget-conscious travelers or those seeking a more social atmosphere, guesthouses and hostels are excellent choices.

These accommodations offer shared dormitory-style rooms or private rooms at affordable rates. Many guesthouses and hostels in Kyoto have communal spaces where travelers can mingle and exchange travel tips.

Machiya

Machiya are traditional townhouses found throughout Kyoto. Some of these machiya have been converted into vacation rental accommodations, allowing guests to experience living in a traditional Japanese home. Staying in a machiya provides a unique opportunity to immerse yourself in the local neighborhood and culture.

Capsule Hotels

Capsule hotels offer compact sleeping pods for single travelers. They are an economical option for those who need a simple and no-frills place to sleep. Capsule hotels usually have separate male and female sections and provide essential amenities.

Business Hotels

Business hotels in Kyoto cater to business travelers but are also suitable for tourists seeking affordable accommodations. These hotels often have compact rooms and basic amenities but are conveniently located near transportation hubs and business districts.

Airbnb and Vacation Rentals

Kyoto has many Airbnb listings and vacation rental properties, offering a range of choices from apartments to traditional homes. Renting a private residence can provide a more homey and personalized experience for travelers.

Dressing Etiquette

Dressing etiquette is an essential aspect of Japanese culture, including when visiting Kyoto. Adhering to appropriate dress codes shows respect for local customs and traditions. Here are some dressing etiquette tips to keep in mind when exploring Kyoto:

Modesty

When visiting temples, shrines, and other traditional sites, it is essential to dress modestly. Avoid wearing revealing clothing, such as shorts, tank tops, or low-cut tops. Instead, opt for clothing that covers your shoulders and knees.

Remove Shoes

In many places, including traditional ryokans, some temples, and private homes, you will be required to remove your shoes before entering. Make sure to wear socks or bring your indoor slippers for comfort.

Easy-to-Remove Shoes

When planning your outfit, consider wearing shoes that are easy to remove and put back on. This will save time and make it more convenient when visiting places with shoe removal customs.

Comfortable Footwear

Kyoto is a city best explored on foot, so comfortable and sturdy shoes are essential. Many temples and shrines have gravel paths or stone walkways, so consider wearing shoes suitable for walking on uneven surfaces.

Cultural Festivals and Events

If you plan to attend cultural festivals, ceremonies, or traditional events, it's a good idea to dress appropriately for the occasion. Some festivals may have specific dress codes, so check in advance if there are any special requirements.

Seasons and Weather

Consider the season and weather when choosing your clothing. Kyoto experiences four distinct seasons, and temperatures can vary significantly. In summer, lightweight and breathable fabrics are recommended, while in winter, you'll need warm clothing.

Formal Occasions

If you plan to dine at a high-end restaurant or attend a formal event in Kyoto, dress appropriately in smart-casual or formal attire. Japanese culture places importance on appearance and presentation, especially in upscale settings.

Tattoos

Keep in mind that visible tattoos may still carry some cultural stigma in Japan, especially in places associated with traditional customs like onsens (hot springs) and public bathhouses. While attitudes are slowly changing, it's best to be discreet about tattoos, especially in such locations.

Language

The primary language spoken in Kyoto, as well as throughout Japan, is Japanese. Japanese is a unique and complex language with its own writing system, grammar, and pronunciation. Here are some key points to know about the Japanese language when visiting Kyoto:

Japanese Script

Japanese uses a combination of three writing scripts: kanji, hiragana, and katakana. Kanji are logographic characters borrowed from Chinese, and they represent meaning and concepts. Hiragana and katakana are syllabaries used for native Japanese words and foreign loanwords, respectively.

English Proficiency

In tourist areas and popular attractions, you will often find signs and information in English to accommodate international visitors. Many hotels, restaurants, and shops catering to tourists will have some English-speaking staff, although the level of English proficiency may vary.

Basic Japanese Phrases

Learning a few basic Japanese phrases can enhance your travel experience and help with everyday interactions. Useful phrases include greetings like "hello" (こんにちは - konnichiwa) and "thank you" (ありがとう - arigatou). Polite expressions like "excuse me" (すみません - sumimasen) and "please" (お願いします - onegaishimasu) are also appreciated.

Communication Tips

When communicating with locals, speaking slowly and clearly can be helpful. While many Japanese people have studied English in school, they may be more comfortable understanding and responding to simple phrases or gestures.

Translation Apps and Phrasebooks

Having a translation app or a pocket phrasebook can be valuable for overcoming language barriers and getting help with communication.

Respectful Communication

Japanese culture places a strong emphasis on politeness and respect in communication. Using appropriate honorifics and bowing as a sign of respect are common customs.

Kanji Challenges

Reading kanji characters can be challenging for those unfamiliar with the script. While many signs and landmarks have English translations, some older or less tourist-oriented places may only display information in Japanese.

Non-Verbal Communication

Non-verbal cues and gestures can also play a significant role in communication. A smile, a nod, or a bow can convey friendliness and understanding even if you don't know the language well.

Currency and Payments

The currency used in Japan is the Japanese Yen (JPY). Here are some important points to know about currency and payments in Kyoto:

Japanese Yen (JPY)

The Japanese Yen comes in various denominations, including coins (1 yen, 5 yen, 10 yen, 50 yen, 100 yen, and 500 yen) and banknotes (1,000 yen, 2,000 yen, 5,000 yen, and 10,000 yen). The 1 yen coin is rarely used in everyday transactions.

Cash is King

While credit cards are widely accepted in major cities and tourist areas, Japan is still largely a cash-based society, especially in smaller businesses and local shops. It's advisable to carry enough cash, particularly when visiting rural or less touristy areas.

ATM Availability

ATMs are readily available in Japan, and you can find them at convenience stores, post offices, banks, and train stations. Many ATMs accept international cards with major networks (Visa, MasterCard, etc.), but it's essential to check with your bank before your trip to ensure your card will work in Japan.

Credit Cards

Major credit cards like Visa, MasterCard, and American Express are generally accepted in hotels, department stores, upscale restaurants, and larger shops. However, some smaller businesses and traditional establishments may only accept cash.

IC Cards

IC cards are rechargeable prepaid cards that offer cashless payments for transportation, convenience stores, vending machines, and some shops. Suica and ICOCA are two widely used IC cards that can be used interchangeably in most regions of Japan, including Kyoto.

Tax-Free Shopping

Foreign tourists visiting Japan are eligible for tax-free shopping for certain items. Look for stores displaying "Tax-Free" signs, and present your passport at the time of purchase to receive a tax refund.

Tipping

Tipping is not customary in Japan and is not expected in restaurants, hotels, or other service establishments. Exceptional service is considered part of the culture and not something to be rewarded with a tip.

Currency Exchange

Currency exchange services are available at major international airports, some hotels, and banks. Rates may vary, so it's a good idea to compare rates before exchanging money. Additionally, ATMs can also be used to withdraw Japanese Yen directly from your home bank account.

Counterfeit Money

Japan is known for its strict anti-counterfeit measures. Make sure to obtain currency from reputable sources and be cautious when receiving large bills to avoid counterfeit money scams.

Safety

Safety is an essential aspect to consider when visiting Kyoto to ensure a pleasant and respectful experience. Here are some safety tips to keep in mind during your trip:

Low Crime Rate

Japan, including Kyoto, is known for its overall safety and low crime rate. However, it's always good to practice common-sense safety precautions, such as keeping your belongings secure, especially in crowded areas and public transportation.

Traffic Safety

In Japan, people generally obey traffic rules, so follow pedestrian signals and use designated crosswalks when crossing the road. Be cautious when walking or cycling on roads, as drivers may not always expect pedestrians or cyclists.

Natural Disasters

Japan is prone to natural disasters, such as earthquakes and typhoons. Familiarize yourself with emergency procedures, and follow instructions from local authorities in case of any natural disaster warnings.

Health and Hygiene: Japan maintains high standards of cleanliness and hygiene. Wash your hands frequently, especially before meals, and use hand sanitizers when necessary.

Etiquette

Bow Greeting

When meeting someone for the first time or showing respect, a slight bow is customary in Japan. The depth of the bow varies depending on the situation.

Quiet and Respectful Behavior

In public places, maintain a quiet and respectful demeanor. Loud conversations and disruptive behavior are generally frowned upon.

Shoes Off Indoors

Many places, such as temples, shrines, traditional ryokans, and private homes, require you to remove your shoes before entering. Follow the lead of others and place your shoes neatly outside.

No Smoking in Public

Smoking is generally not allowed on the streets in Japan. Use designated smoking areas or smoking rooms provided in certain establishments.

Eating and Drinking Etiquette

When dining in traditional restaurants, wait for everyone to be served before starting your meal. Slurping noodles is considered acceptable and even a compliment to the chef.

Public Transportation

Be mindful of others on public transportation and avoid talking on the phone or playing music loudly. Refrain from eating or drinking on buses, subways, and trains, unless it is explicitly allowed.

Tattoos

Tattoos may be associated with the yakuza (Japanese organized crime) and are sometimes stigmatized in traditional settings. Covering tattoos with clothing or bandages is recommended, especially in places like onsens and public bathhouses.

Gift-Giving

If you wish to offer gifts, especially when invited to someone's home or when leaving a ryokan, small souvenirs from your home country are appreciated.

Travel Insurance

Travel insurance is an essential aspect of any trip, including when visiting Kyoto or any other destination. It provides financial protection and peace of mind in case of unforeseen events or emergencies that may occur during your travels. Here are some key points to consider about travel insurance:

Coverage Types

Travel insurance typically offers various types of coverage, including:

- **Trip Cancellation or Interruption:** Reimburses non-refundable trip costs if you need to cancel or cut short your trip due to covered reasons, such as illness, injury, or unforeseen circumstances.

- **Medical Coverage:** Covers medical expenses and emergency medical evacuations during your trip.

- **Lost or Delayed Baggage:** Provides compensation for lost, stolen, or delayed baggage and belongings.

- **Travel Delay:** Offers reimbursement for additional expenses incurred due to flight delays or trip interruptions.

- **Personal Liability:** Covers costs associated with accidental damage or injury to others during your travels.

Check Your Policy

Before purchasing travel insurance, carefully review the policy to understand what it covers and any exclusions or limitations. Policies can vary, so make sure it meets your specific needs and the type of trip you have planned.

Destination Coverage

Ensure that the travel insurance policy covers the destination you are visiting (in this case, Kyoto, Japan). Some policies may have limitations or exclusions for certain countries or regions.

Pre-Existing Conditions

If you have any pre-existing medical conditions, check if the policy covers them. Some policies may offer coverage for pre-existing conditions if you meet specific requirements, while others may exclude them altogether.

Duration and Extending Coverage

Select a policy that covers the entire duration of your trip, from departure to return. If you plan to extend your trip, check if you can extend the coverage accordingly.

Travel Insurance Providers

Numerous insurance companies offer travel insurance plans. Compare plans, coverage, and prices from different providers to find the one that best suits your needs.

Emergency Contact Information

Keep the travel insurance provider's contact information and policy details readily accessible during your trip. This includes any emergency helpline numbers that may be provided in the policy.

Purchase in Advance

It's recommended to purchase travel insurance soon after booking your trip. Some policies may have specific coverage limitations if purchased close to the departure date.

KYOTO TEMPLES

Kyoto is renowned for its numerous temples, each with its own unique charm and historical significance. Here are some of the most notable temples you should consider visiting in Kyoto:

Kinkaku-ji (Golden Pavilion)

Kinkaku-ji, also known as the Golden Pavilion, is a breathtaking Zen Buddhist temple located in Kyoto, Japan. It is one of the city's most iconic landmarks and a UNESCO World Heritage Site. The temple's distinctive feature is its upper two floors, which are entirely covered in shimmering gold leaf, creating an awe-inspiring sight that leaves visitors in awe. Kinkaku-ji's reflection in the tranquil pond that surrounds it adds to its allure, making it a must-visit attraction for travelers from all around the world.

The history of Kinkaku-ji dates back to the late 14th century when it was originally built as a retirement villa for Ashikaga Yoshimitsu, a powerful shogun during the Muromachi period. Following Yoshimitsu's death, in accordance with his will, the villa was converted into a Zen temple by his successor. Throughout the years, the temple has undergone several renovations and restorations, but its striking golden exterior has remained a symbol of spiritual beauty and artistic elegance.

Approaching Kinkaku-ji, visitors are greeted by meticulously manicured gardens that lead to the temple's entrance. The lush greenery and carefully arranged landscape create a serene atmosphere that enhances the temple's spiritual significance. Upon reaching the temple's edge, one is met with an unparalleled view of the Golden Pavilion, brilliantly reflecting on the calm waters of Kyoko-chi Pond. The sight of the gilded temple shimmering in the sunlight against the backdrop of clear blue skies or autumn foliage is nothing short of magical.

The three floors of Kinkaku-ji represent different architectural styles—Shinden, Samurai, and Zen—and each floor embodies a unique cultural influence. The first floor features wooden pillars and white plaster walls, in contrast to the resplendent gold leaf above. The second floor showcases samurai warrior culture with its simple design and dark wooden exterior. The topmost floor, adorned in exquisite gold leaf, pays homage to Zen Buddhism and the pursuit of enlightenment.

Visitors can stroll through the garden's winding paths, enjoy the serene atmosphere, and admire Kinkaku-ji from various viewpoints. The beauty of the temple is accentuated throughout the year with cherry blossoms in spring, vibrant colors in autumn, and peaceful snowscapes in winter.

Kinkaku-ji stands as a symbol of Japan's rich cultural heritage, epitomizing the harmonious blend of nature, art, and spirituality. Its reflection on the pond not only adds to its allure but also symbolizes the importance of inner reflection and finding beauty in both the tangible and the ephemeral. For those seeking a profound cultural experience and a moment of wonderment, Kinkaku-ji is an unmissable destination that leaves an indelible impression on every visitor's heart and soul. Here's more information about Kinkaku-ji:

Architecture

The main highlight of Kinkaku-ji is the stunning Golden Pavilion, a three-story building covered in gold leaf. The first floor is built in the Shinden-zukuri architectural style, reminiscent of aristocratic residences during the Heian period. The second floor showcases the elegant samurai aesthetic, while the top floor is influenced by Zen Buddhism with its minimalistic design and golden phoenix statue.

Kyoko-chi Pond and Gardens

Kinkaku-ji is surrounded by beautifully landscaped gardens and a large pond called Kyoko-chi, which mirrors the Golden Pavilion. The garden features walking paths, stone bridges, lush vegetation, and meticulously maintained scenery that reflects the changing seasons.

Tea House

Within the temple complex, there is a traditional teahouse where visitors can enjoy a cup of matcha (powdered green tea) and experience a Japanese tea ceremony. The teahouse offers a serene setting overlooking the garden.

Zen Buddhism

Kinkaku-ji is affiliated with the Rinzai sect of Zen Buddhism. The temple follows the Zen philosophy, emphasizing meditation, self-discipline, and enlightenment. The serene atmosphere and picturesque surroundings make it an ideal place for contemplation and reflection.

Cultural Significance

Kinkaku-ji holds cultural and historical significance as a symbol of Kyoto's rich heritage. Its striking appearance and harmony with nature have inspired artists, writers, and travelers for centuries, making it a popular subject in literature, poetry, and visual arts.

Visitor Experience

Kinkaku-ji attracts a large number of visitors, particularly during peak tourist seasons. To preserve the delicate structure and surroundings, access to the interior of the Golden Pavilion is not permitted. However, visitors can walk around the temple, enjoy the gardens, and take memorable photos from designated viewpoints.

Ryoan-ji

Ryoan-ji is home to one of the most famous Zen rock gardens in Japan. The simplicity of its design, consisting of 15 rocks arranged on white gravel, encourages meditation and reflection. Take some time to sit and contemplate the beauty of this serene space.

Ginkaku-ji (Silver Pavilion)

Ginkaku-ji, also known as the Silver Pavilion, is a Zen Buddhist temple located in the eastern part of Kyoto. Although it's called the Silver Pavilion, it was never actually covered in silver. However, its elegant architecture and beautiful gardens make it a popular destination for visitors. Here's more information about Ginkaku-ji:

History

Ginkaku-ji was originally built in 1482 as a retirement villa for the shogun Ashikaga Yoshimasa, the grandson of the shogun who built Kinkaku-ji (Golden Pavilion). After Yoshimasa's death, the villa was converted into a Zen temple.

Unlike the original plan to cover it in silver, only the interior of the pavilion was decorated with silver.

Architecture

Ginkaku-ji features a two-story wooden pavilion known as the Silver Pavilion. The upper floor showcases the shoin-zukuri architectural style, characterized by tatami mat flooring, sliding doors, and intricate woodworking. The lower floor has a more rustic appearance. The design of the pavilion represents the Higashiyama culture, a refined aesthetic style popular during the Muromachi period.

Togudo Hall

Adjacent to the Silver Pavilion is the Togudo Hall, which houses statues of Buddhist deities. The hall features beautiful painted sliding doors and offers a glimpse into the religious practices of the temple.

Gardens

Ginkaku-ji is famous for its meticulously designed gardens that complement the natural surroundings. The main garden features a sand mound called the Moon Viewing Platform, which is designed to resemble Mt. Fuji. Other garden elements include carefully placed rocks, moss, and meticulously pruned trees. The garden is especially enchanting during autumn when the vibrant colors of the foliage add to its beauty.

Path of Philosophy

The approach to Ginkaku-ji is part of the famous Philosopher's Path, a picturesque pedestrian path that follows a canal lined with cherry trees. Walking this path, particularly during cherry blossom season in spring, offers a scenic and tranquil experience.

Tea House and Tea Garden

Within the temple grounds, there is a tea house called Sekkatei, where visitors can enjoy matcha tea and traditional Japanese sweets. The tea house overlooks a serene tea garden, providing a peaceful setting to relax and appreciate the aesthetics of the temple.

Zen Buddhism

Ginkaku-ji is associated with the Zen Buddhism of the Rinzai sect. The temple embodies the Zen principles of simplicity, tranquility, and appreciation of nature. The serene environment of the temple and its gardens reflects the Zen philosophy.

Kiyomizu-dera

Kiyomizu-dera is one of Kyoto's most iconic and celebrated temples. Its name translates to "Pure Water Temple," referring to the Otawa Waterfall that runs through the temple grounds. Here's more information about Kiyomizu-dera:

History

Kiyomizu-dera was first established in 778 CE and has a history spanning over 1,200 years. The temple complex went through various reconstructions and expansions over the centuries. The current buildings date back to 1633, reconstructed by the Tokugawa shogunate.

Architecture

Kiyomizu-dera is known for its wooden terrace, called the Kiyomizu Stage, which juts out from the main hall. The stage offers panoramic views of Kyoto city and is supported by 13-meter tall wooden pillars without the use of nails. It is an architectural marvel and a symbol of Japanese craftsmanship.

Otawa Waterfall

The Otawa Waterfall is located within the temple grounds, and visitors can drink from the three streams of water believed to have different benefits—success in studies, health, and finding love. Each stream has its own designated spot where visitors use cups attached to long poles to collect the water.

Jishu Shrine

Jishu Shrine, located within the temple complex, is dedicated to the deity of love and matchmaking. The shrine houses two "love stones" placed a few meters apart, and it is said that if visitors can walk between the stones with their eyes closed successfully, they will find love.

Seasonal Beauty

Kiyomizu-dera is breathtaking in every season. During spring, cherry blossoms adorn the temple grounds, creating a stunning backdrop. In autumn, the vibrant foliage surrounding the temple transforms the area into a kaleidoscope of colors. These seasons attract many visitors, and the temple is particularly popular during these times.

Light-Up Events

Kiyomizu-dera holds special light-up events a few times a year, where the temple and its surroundings are beautifully illuminated in the evening. These events offer a magical atmosphere and a chance to see the temple in a different light.

Kiyomizu-zaka and Sannenzaka Streets

The approach to Kiyomizu-dera temple is lined with traditional shops and cafes. Kiyomizu-zaka and Sannenzaka streets offer a nostalgic atmosphere and are popular spots for strolling, shopping for souvenirs, and sampling local snacks.

Sanjusangendo

This temple is famous for its impressive main hall, which houses 1,001 life-sized statues of Kannon, the Buddhist goddess of mercy. The sight of the statues is awe-inspiring and offers a unique cultural experience.

Nanzen-ji

This temple complex features several sub-temples, beautiful gardens, and a massive brick aqueduct. Explore the peaceful grounds and enjoy the blend of nature and architecture.

The Byōdō-in Temple

The Byōdō-in Temple is deserving of a visit because it has numerous distinctive structures, sanctuaries, and artwork. The Phoenix Hall (Hoo-do), with its two gables decorated with metal phoenixes, is one of the attractions. In addition to an impressive gilded statue of Amida, this appealing hall has frescoes from the 11th century as well as an altar and ceiling with bronze and mother-of-pearl inlays.

Sanjūsangen-dō Temple

The name of the temple, Sanjsangen-d (Rengyoin Temple), which is also known as the Temple of the 33 recesses, comes from its rather unusual façade, which is divided into 33 (sanjusan) recesses to symbolize the concept that Kannon, the Goddess of Mercy, could assume 33 different personifications. The current long building was created in 1266 after a fire devastated the original structure that was erected in 1164. The numerous holes that arrowheads have left in the building's old supports and beams, which once served as a center for archery training, are still visible proof of its former significance.

Nishi Honganji Temple

The primary temple of the original Jodo-Shinshu sect, Nishi Honganji shrine, is a beautiful example of a Buddhist structure. The Main Hall, or Hondo, is among the highlights. This beautiful structure, which was rebuilt in 1760, is noteworthy for its many chambers adorned with murals on gold backdrops and its numerous significant sculptures, some of which date back as far as the sixth century.

Tofuku-ji Temple

Tofuku-ji Temple is a significant Zen Buddhist temple located in southern Kyoto. It is renowned for its beautiful gardens, impressive architecture, and stunning autumn foliage views. Here's more information about Tofuku-ji Temple:

History

Tofuku-ji Temple was founded in 1236 during the Kamakura period by the influential monk Enni Ben'en. The temple was established as the head temple of the Tofuku-ji school of the Rinzai sect of Zen Buddhism. Over the centuries, the temple has undergone various reconstructions and expansions, maintaining its importance in the Zen Buddhist tradition.

Sanmon Gate

The Sanmon Gate of Tofuku-ji is one of the largest and oldest Zen gates in Japan. It dates back to the early 15th century and serves as the main entrance to the temple. The gate is an impressive structure with intricate architectural details and offers a symbolic entrance into the world of Zen Buddhism.

Hojo and Gardens

The Hojo is the main hall of Tofuku-ji Temple, which houses the temple's principal objects of worship. The hall is surrounded by stunning gardens, including the Kaisan-do Garden, Tsuten-kyo Bridge, and Tofuku-ji's renowned autumn foliage garden. The gardens are meticulously landscaped, providing a tranquil and picturesque setting for contemplation and reflection.

Autumn Foliage

Tofuku-ji Temple is particularly famous for its autumn foliage, attracting numerous visitors during the fall season. The temple's Tsuten-kyo Bridge, spanning across a valley, offers a breathtaking view of the vibrant red and golden leaves of the surrounding maple trees. The autumn colors at Tofuku-ji are considered among the most spectacular in Kyoto.

Zen Meditation

Tofuku-ji Temple offers Zen meditation experiences for visitors who wish to learn and practice meditation. These sessions provide an opportunity to experience the calming and introspective nature of Zen Buddhism under the guidance of experienced Zen practitioners.

Cultural Treasures

Tofuku-ji Temple houses several important cultural assets, including Zen Buddhist paintings, calligraphy, and historical artifacts. The temple's rich collection reflects the history and artistic heritage of Zen Buddhism in Japan.

Tofuku-ji Temple Town

The area surrounding Tofuku-ji Temple, known as Tofuku-ji Temple Town, features traditional machiya (wooden townhouses) and local shops. Exploring the town allows visitors to experience the atmosphere of old Kyoto and discover hidden gems like traditional tea houses and small temples.

Gio-ji Temple

Gio-ji Temple is a small, secluded temple located in the Arashiyama district of Kyoto, Japan. It is known for its tranquil and mystical atmosphere, moss-covered grounds, and serene natural surroundings. Here's more information about Gio-ji Temple:

History

Gio-ji Temple was originally established in the 11th century by a noblewoman named Gio, who was a former court dancer. Gio became a nun after being rejected by her lover, and she built the temple as a place of retreat and prayer. The temple has undergone renovations and restorations over the centuries, but it still retains its serene and intimate ambiance.

Moss Garden

The main highlight of Gio-ji Temple is its mesmerizing moss garden. The temple grounds are covered in various species of moss, creating a lush and enchanting carpet of green. The mossy scenery, along with the thatched-roofed hut and stone path, contributes to a serene and picturesque setting that evokes a sense of tranquility and harmony with nature.

Jizo Statues

Within the temple grounds, you can find numerous small Jizo statues, which are stone figures representing the bodhisattva Jizo. These statues are often adorned with red bibs and hats, representing the belief that Jizo protects and guides departed souls. The sight of these statues amidst the mossy landscape adds to the temple's mystical atmosphere.

Autumn Foliage

While Gio-ji Temple is not as renowned for autumn foliage as some other temples in Kyoto, the surrounding area of Arashiyama offers beautiful foliage views during the fall season. Visiting Gio-ji Temple in autumn allows you to enjoy the serene environment while being surrounded by the vibrant colors of the changing leaves.

Intimate Setting

Gio-ji Temple's smaller size and secluded location contribute to its intimate and peaceful setting. Unlike some of Kyoto's larger and more crowded temples, Gio-ji Temple provides a more serene and personal experience, allowing visitors to appreciate the beauty of nature and the temple's unique atmosphere.

Zen Buddhism

Gio-ji Temple is associated with Zen Buddhism, a school of Buddhism known for its emphasis on meditation and mindfulness. The temple's peaceful surroundings and minimalist design reflect the principles of Zen Buddhism, offering visitors an opportunity for quiet contemplation and introspection.

Nearby Attractions

Gio-ji Temple is located in close proximity to other popular attractions in the Arashiyama area, such as the iconic Bamboo Grove and the picturesque Togetsukyo Bridge. Exploring these nearby sites before or after visiting Gio-ji Temple allows for a more comprehensive experience of the region.

Adashino Nenbutsu-ji Temple

Adashino Nenbutsu-ji Temple is a unique and captivating temple located in the outskirts of Kyoto. It is known for its vast collection of small stone statues and its serene and contemplative atmosphere. Here's more information about Adashino Nenbutsu-ji Temple:

History and Significance

Adashino Nenbutsu-ji Temple has a profound historical background and is associated with memorializing the departed. It was originally established in the 9th century as a place for memorial services for the souls of those who died without proper burials during turbulent times in Kyoto's history. The temple's primary purpose is to honor and pray for the repose of the deceased.

Stone Statues

Adashino Nenbutsu-ji Temple is known for its vast collection of small stone statues, called nenbutsu. These statues represent the souls of the departed and are placed throughout the temple grounds. It is estimated that there are over 8,000 stone statues in total, each one uniquely carved and arranged, creating a solemn and haunting atmosphere.

Memorial Rituals

The temple holds memorial rituals to pray for the repose of the departed. One of the most notable rituals is the Tsukinami Kuyo, which takes place on the 15th of each month. During this ceremony, monks chant sutras, and visitors have the opportunity to light incense and pay their respects to the deceased.

Bamboo Grove and Stone Lanterns

The temple grounds of Adashino Nenbutsu-ji feature a serene bamboo grove, providing a tranquil backdrop to the stone statues. Along the pathways, you can also find rows of stone lanterns, further enhancing the spiritual ambiance of the temple.

Surrounding Area

Adashino Nenbutsu-ji Temple is located in a picturesque area surrounded by nature. It is situated near the Arashiyama district and the Sagano Bamboo Forest, making it convenient to explore these nearby attractions as well.

Adashino Festival

Adashino Nenbutsu-ji Temple holds an annual event called the Adashino Festival. This festival, held in August, includes ceremonies, traditional dances, and rituals to remember and honor the spirits of the departed.

Contemplative Environment

Adashino Nenbutsu-ji Temple offers a serene and contemplative environment for visitors. The combination of the stone statues, bamboo grove, and the temple's historical significance creates a unique atmosphere that invites quiet reflection and introspection.

Kokedera (Moss Temple)

Kokedera, also known as Saiho-ji Temple, is a serene and enchanting Buddhist temple located in the western part of Kyoto. It is renowned for its magnificent moss garden, which is considered one of the most beautiful and well-preserved in Japan. Here's more information about Kokedera:

History

Kokedera was founded in the 14th century by the monk Muso Soseki, a prominent figure in Japanese Zen Buddhism. The temple's main hall, called Hojo, was constructed as a place for meditation and religious study. Over the centuries, Kokedera gained fame for its stunning moss garden, attracting visitors from far and wide.

Moss Garden

The moss garden of Kokedera is its main highlight and covers a large area within the temple grounds. The garden features over 120 varieties of moss, creating a lush and vibrant carpet of green. The mosses thrive due to the temple's unique environment, which includes ample shade, moisture, and careful maintenance.

Zen Meditation

Kokedera offers visitors the opportunity to participate in Zen meditation, known as Zazen. Prior to entering the moss garden, visitors are guided through a meditation session led by the temple's monks. This allows visitors to experience the serene and contemplative atmosphere that Kokedera embodies.

UNESCO World Heritage

Kokedera, along with 16 other monuments in Kyoto, is designated as a UNESCO World Heritage site. It is recognized for its historical and cultural significance, representing the Zen Buddhist tradition and the harmonious integration of nature and architecture.

Visitors by Appointment

Due to its delicate moss garden and the desire to maintain a serene atmosphere, Kokedera requires visitors to make advance reservations. Visitors must send a letter requesting permission to visit the temple and receive a designated date and time for their visit. This unique entry process ensures that the temple remains peaceful and uncrowded.

Tea Ceremony

Kokedera is also known for its traditional tea ceremonies. Visitors can participate in a tea ceremony experience, where they can observe or partake in the art of tea preparation and enjoy a bowl of matcha tea in a tranquil setting.

Buddhist Scriptures

Kokedera houses a significant collection of Buddhist scriptures and historical documents. The temple's library contains a vast number of ancient texts, some of which are designated as national treasures or important cultural properties.

Otagi Nenbutsu-ji Temple

Otagi Nenbutsu-ji Temple is a hidden gem located in the Arashiyama district of Kyoto. It is known for its whimsical and charming collection of over 1,200 stone statues, each with its own distinct expression and personality. Here's more information about Otagi Nenbutsu-ji Temple:

History

Otagi Nenbutsu-ji Temple was originally founded in the 8th century by Emperor Shomu, but it fell into disrepair over the years. In 1922, a prominent Buddhist sculptor named Kocho Nishimura led a restoration project and added the unique collection of stone statues that the temple is now famous for.

Stone Statues

The highlight of Otagi Nenbutsu-ji Temple is its extensive collection of stone statues known as rakan, which represent the disciples of Buddha. Each statue has its own facial expression, posing in various whimsical and humorous ways. Some are smiling, some are frowning, and others are making comical gestures, creating a lively and playful atmosphere.

Restoration Efforts

The stone statues at Otagi Nenbutsu-ji Temple were added during the restoration project in the 20th century. Local residents and temple supporters contributed to the creation of the statues, which were carved by hand. This collaborative effort adds a unique and community-oriented aspect to the temple's history.

Serene Setting

Otagi Nenbutsu-ji Temple is situated in a tranquil and wooded area, away from the bustling tourist areas of Kyoto. The peaceful surroundings enhance the contemplative and reflective atmosphere of the temple, making it a peaceful retreat for visitors.

Seasonal Beauty

Otagi Nenbutsu-ji Temple offers different perspectives throughout the year. During spring, cherry blossoms adorn the temple grounds, providing a picturesque setting. In autumn, the foliage surrounding the temple takes on vibrant colors, creating a stunning backdrop for the stone statues.

Walking Meditation

The temple grounds provide a serene environment for walking meditation. Visitors can take a leisurely stroll among the stone statues, allowing them to engage in mindfulness and reflection while enjoying the whimsical artistry of the sculptures.

Off-the-Beaten-Path Experience

Otagi Nenbutsu-ji Temple is often considered a hidden gem in Kyoto. Due to its location away from major tourist attractions, it offers a quieter and more intimate experience compared to other popular temples in the city.

Hosen-in Temple

Hosen-in Temple is a serene Buddhist temple located in the mountainous area of Ohara, just north of Kyoto. It is known for its beautiful gardens, tranquil atmosphere, and stunning autumn foliage. Here's more information about Hosen-in Temple:

History

Hosen-in Temple has a history that dates back over 1,200 years. It was originally established as a Tendai Buddhist temple in the Heian period and later became affiliated with the Soto Zen sect. The temple has witnessed many renovations and additions over the centuries, but it has retained its traditional and peaceful ambiance.

Gardens

Hosen-in Temple is renowned for its meticulously maintained gardens, which offer a sense of serenity and harmony with nature. The main garden, known as Suirokaku, features a large pond adorned with beautiful lotus flowers and surrounded by lush greenery. The garden is particularly breathtaking during the autumn season when the vibrant colors of the maple trees reflect in the tranquil waters.

Hojo (Main Hall)

The Hojo is the main hall of Hosen-in Temple and serves as the focal point of the temple complex. It houses a few important artifacts, including a beautiful sliding door painting attributed to the famed artist Kano Eigaku. Visitors can enter the Hojo and experience the tranquil atmosphere while appreciating the artistic and architectural details.

Maple Trees and Autumn Foliage

Hosen-in Temple is renowned for its breathtaking display of autumn foliage. The temple's maple trees transform into a vivid palette of red, orange, and gold, creating a magical and serene atmosphere. Visitors can explore the temple grounds, enjoying the vibrant colors and peaceful surroundings during the autumn season.

Stone Garden

Hosen-in Temple features a unique stone garden called Karesansui, also known as a dry landscape garden. This minimalist garden style uses carefully placed rocks and gravel to represent natural elements such as mountains, rivers, and waterfalls. The stone garden provides a meditative space for contemplation and reflection.

Tea Room

Hosen-in Temple has a traditional tea room where visitors can experience a Japanese tea ceremony. The serene environment of the tea room and the ritual of preparing and drinking matcha tea offer a tranquil and immersive cultural experience.

Off-the-Beaten-Path Location

Hosen-in Temple is located in the peaceful countryside of Ohara, away from the bustling city center of Kyoto. Its secluded location adds to its charm and provides a sense of serenity and tranquility that is distinct from the more popular tourist spots.

KYOTO SHRINES

Kyoto is home to numerous shrines, each with its own unique charm and historical significance. Here are some of the notable shrines you should consider visiting in Kyoto:

Fushimi Inari Taisha

Fushimi Inari Taisha is a famous Shinto shrine located in the southern part of Kyoto. It is renowned for its thousands of vibrant red torii gates, which create a mesmerizing tunnel-like pathway through the forested Mount Inari. Here's more information about Fushimi Inari Taisha:

History and Significance

Fushimi Inari Taisha is dedicated to the Shinto deity Inari, who is revered as the god of rice, agriculture, and prosperity. The shrine dates back to the 8th century and has been an important pilgrimage site for worshippers seeking good fortune, success in business, and bountiful harvests.

Torii Gates

One of the most iconic features of Fushimi Inari Taisha is its thousands of vibrant red torii gates, known as "Senbon Torii." These gates were donated by individuals and businesses as a gesture of gratitude or to seek blessings from Inari. Walking through the torii gates creates a unique and immersive experience as you traverse the winding paths of Mount Inari.

Hiking Trails

Fushimi Inari Taisha offers a network of hiking trails that lead up the mountain. The main trail is a 4-kilometer loop that takes you through the torii gates, past smaller shrines, and offers scenic viewpoints along the way. The trails are well-marked, and visitors can choose to hike a shorter section or explore the entire loop, depending on their time and energy.

Fox Statues

Inari is often depicted with foxes, which are considered sacred messengers of the deity. You will encounter numerous fox statues throughout the shrine grounds, many of which are adorned with red bibs, representing Inari's protection and favor.

Sub-shrines and Offerings

Along the paths of Fushimi Inari Taisha, you will find smaller sub-shrines dedicated to various gods and deities. These sub-shrines often feature unique statues, prayer areas, and opportunities for visitors to make offerings or purchase omamori (protective amulets).

Cultural Events

Fushimi Inari Taisha is also the site of various cultural events throughout the year. The most notable event is the annual Kitsune-no-Yomeiri (Fox Wedding) ceremony held in early February, where participants dress in traditional wedding attire and take part in a procession.

Yasaka Shrine

Yasaka Shrine, also known as Gion Shrine, is a prominent Shinto shrine located in the Gion district of Kyoto. It is one of the city's most well-known and popular shrines, attracting visitors and locals alike. Here's more information about Yasaka Shrine:

History

Yasaka Shrine has a long history that dates back over 1,350 years. It was originally established in the 7th century and was dedicated to the deity Susanoo-no-Mikoto, who is believed to protect against illness and bring good fortune. The shrine has been an important site for religious ceremonies and festivals throughout the centuries.

Gion Festival

Yasaka Shrine is closely associated with the annual Gion Matsuri, one of Japan's most famous festivals. The festival takes place throughout the month of July and features processions, performances, and elaborate floats called "yamaboko." The highlight of the festival is the Yamaboko Junko, a grand parade through the streets of Kyoto, attracting millions of visitors.

Architecture

The main hall of Yasaka Shrine, called the Honden, features traditional Shinto architectural style with a distinctive vermillion color. The Honden is surrounded by several other buildings, including the stage for performances and ceremonies. The shrine's architecture reflects the grandeur and elegance of traditional Japanese design.

Lanterns

Yasaka Shrine is known for its numerous lanterns, which adorn the shrine grounds and create a beautiful ambiance, especially in the evening. The lanterns are lit during festivals and events, adding to the shrine's enchanting atmosphere.

Gion District

Yasaka Shrine is located in the heart of the Gion district, one of Kyoto's most historic and picturesque areas. The district is famous for its traditional machiya houses, teahouses, and geisha culture. It offers a unique blend of history, culture, and entertainment.

Hanami (Cherry Blossom Viewing)

During spring, Yasaka Shrine's surrounding area, particularly Maruyama Park, becomes a popular spot for hanami, the tradition of cherry blossom viewing. The shrine's cherry trees create a stunning backdrop, attracting visitors who gather to enjoy the beauty of the blossoms.

New Year's Celebration

Like many other Shinto shrines, Yasaka Shrine holds special events during the New Year period. Many people visit the shrine to pray for a prosperous year and participate in traditional rituals and ceremonies.

Heian Shrine

Heian Shrine, also known as Heian Jingu, is a Shinto shrine located in Kyoto. It was built in 1895 to commemorate the 1,100th anniversary of the establishment of Kyoto as the capital of Japan. Here's more information about Heian Shrine:

Architecture

Heian Shrine replicates the design of the original Imperial Palace from the Heian period (794-1185). The main gate, known as the Ōtenmon, is a large wooden structure adorned with intricate carvings. The shrine's main hall, or Shinden, is a scale replica of the original Imperial Palace's main hall. The vibrant vermilion color and the large courtyard create a striking sight.

Gardens

Heian Shrine is known for its expansive gardens, which cover approximately 33,000 square meters. The gardens are designed in a style reminiscent of the Heian period and include various elements such as ponds, bridges, rock formations, and carefully placed vegetation. The gardens are particularly beautiful during cherry blossom season and autumn foliage season.

Inner Shrine

Within the shrine complex, there is an inner sanctuary called Shin-en. This area includes a large pond called Byakko-ike, which is shaped like the character for "heart" in Japanese. Visitors can cross the bridge and take in the serene atmosphere of the pond and its surrounding greenery.

Peaceful Environment

Heian Shrine is located in a relatively quieter area of Kyoto, away from the hustle and bustle of the city center. The spacious grounds and well-maintained gardens offer a peaceful and tranquil atmosphere, making it an ideal place for relaxation and contemplation.

Festivals and Events

Heian Shrine hosts various festivals and events throughout the year. One of the most famous events is the Jidai Matsuri, held on October 22nd, where participants dressed in historical costumes parade from the Imperial Palace to Heian Shrine to commemorate Kyoto's rich history. The shrine also hosts traditional ceremonies and rituals during New Year's and other significant occasions.

Culture and History

Heian Shrine is dedicated to the spirits of Emperor Kammu and Emperor Komei, who were instrumental in the establishment and development of Kyoto. It serves as a reminder of Kyoto's historical significance and pays homage to the city's illustrious past.

Kitano Tenmangu Shrine

Kitano Tenmangu Shrine is a Shinto shrine located in the northwest part of Kyoto. It is dedicated to Sugawara no

Michizane, a scholar and politician from the Heian period who is revered as the deity of learning and academic success. Here's more information about Kitano Tenmangu Shrine:

History

Kitano Tenmangu Shrine was established in 947 CE and is one of the oldest and most prestigious shrines in Kyoto. It was built to enshrine Sugawara no Michizane after his death and has since become a popular site for students and academics to pray for success in their studies.

Sugawara no Michizane

Sugawara no Michizane was a prominent scholar, poet, and politician of the Heian period. He was known for his intellect and contributions to Japanese literature. After his death, he was deified as Tenjin, the god of scholarship and learning. Kitano Tenmangu Shrine is one of the many shrines across Japan dedicated to him.

Architecture

The main hall of Kitano Tenmangu Shrine showcases traditional Shinto architecture with its distinct red color and intricate wooden carvings. The entrance gate, called the Chumon, and the worship hall, known as the Haiden, are also notable architectural features of the shrine.

Plum Blossoms

Kitano Tenmangu Shrine is renowned for its plum blossoms. With over 2,000 plum trees of different varieties, the shrine's plum garden (Baikasai) is particularly popular during February when the plum blossoms are in full bloom. The Baikasai festival takes place annually and features tea ceremonies, traditional performances, and other celebratory activities.

Market and Festivals

On the 25th of every month, the shrine hosts Tenjin-san, a traditional flea market where vendors sell various goods such as antiques, crafts, clothing, and food. Additionally, the shrine holds several festivals throughout the year, including the Tenjin-sai festival in July and the Tsukimi festival (moon viewing) in September.

Cultural and Educational Events

Kitano Tenmangu Shrine organizes cultural events and activities related to art, calligraphy, and traditional Japanese culture. Visitors can participate in workshops, exhibitions, and performances to deepen their understanding of Japanese traditions and artistic practices.

Study and Exam Prayers

Many students visit Kitano Tenmangu Shrine to pray for success in their studies or exams. The shrine's association with learning and academia makes it a significant place for students seeking blessings and inspiration.

Kamigamo Shrine

Kamigamo Shrine, also known as Kamigamo-jinja, is an ancient Shinto shrine located in the northern part of Kyoto. It is one of the oldest and most important shrines in the city, with a history that dates back over 1,300 years. Here's more information about Kamigamo Shrine:

History and Significance

Kamigamo Shrine was established in the 7th century and is dedicated to the deity Kamo Wake-Ikazuchi-no-Kami. The shrine holds great historical and cultural significance as it has been associated with the Kamo clan, a powerful clan of priests and warriors in ancient Kyoto. It played a vital role in protecting the city from evil spirits and natural disasters.

Architecture

The main hall of Kamigamo Shrine, called the Honden, is designated as a National Treasure of Japan. It showcases the traditional Shinto architectural style known as nagare-zukuri, characterized by its curved roofline. The Honden and other structures within the shrine complex feature a rustic and elegant design that reflects the shrine's long history.

Kamogawa River

Kamigamo Shrine is situated along the banks of the Kamo River, which is believed to be a sacred river in Shinto mythology. The river and the surrounding natural landscape create a serene and picturesque environment, offering a peaceful retreat from the urban areas of Kyoto.

Setsubun Festival

One of the most popular events at Kamigamo Shrine is the Setsubun Festival, held on February 3rd each year. The festival marks the beginning of spring according to the lunar calendar. Participants throw roasted soybeans to drive away evil spirits and bring good fortune for the year ahead.

Aoi Matsuri Procession

Kamigamo Shrine is closely associated with the annual Aoi Matsuri, one of Kyoto's three major festivals. The festival takes place on May 15th and features a grand procession that starts at the Kyoto Imperial Palace and ends at Kamigamo

Shrine. Participants dress in Heian-period costumes and parade through the streets of Kyoto, attracting thousands of spectators.

Natural Setting

Kamigamo Shrine is surrounded by a sacred forest known as Tadasu no Mori. The forest is considered a spiritual sanctuary and is believed to be the dwelling place of gods and spirits. Visitors can take a stroll through the forest, enjoying the peaceful atmosphere and connecting with nature.

Omokaru-ishi

One of the unique features of Kamigamo Shrine is the Omokaru-ishi, or "weighing stone." It is a large stone with two handles that visitors can lift to determine their fortunes. It is believed that lifting the stone with ease brings good luck, while struggling to lift it may indicate challenges ahead.

Shimogamo Shrine

Shimogamo Shrine, also known as Shimogamo-jinja, is a historic Shinto shrine located in the northern part of Kyoto. Along with its counterpart, Kamigamo Shrine, it forms the Kamo Shrines, which are collectively designated as UNESCO World Heritage sites. Here's more information about Shimogamo Shrine:

History and Significance

Shimogamo Shrine has a history that spans over 2,000 years, making it one of the oldest shrines in Kyoto. It is dedicated to the deity Kamo Wake-Ikazuchi-no-Kami, who is believed to protect the city from disasters and bring good fortune. The shrine has deep roots in Shinto traditions and plays a significant role in Kyoto's spiritual and cultural heritage.

Architecture

The main hall of Shimogamo Shrine, called the Honden, features the distinctive nagare-zukuri architectural style commonly found in Shinto shrines. It has a gabled roof, wooden pillars, and an open front, reflecting the simplicity and reverence of Shinto beliefs. The surrounding structures within the shrine complex maintain a traditional aesthetic that harmonizes with the natural environment.

Tadasu no Mori

Shimogamo Shrine is located within Tadasu no Mori, a sacred forest that has been preserved for centuries. This dense forest is considered a spiritual sanctuary and is believed to house divine spirits. It provides a serene and peaceful atmosphere for visitors to explore and connect with nature.

Annual Festivals

Shimogamo Shrine hosts several annual festivals, the most significant being the Aoi Matsuri. Held on May 15th, this festival features a grand procession from the Kyoto Imperial Palace to Shimogamo Shrine. Participants, dressed in Heian-period costumes, parade through the streets of Kyoto, offering prayers and blessings for a good harvest and protection against disasters.

Mitarashi Festival

The Mitarashi Festival, held in July, is another popular event at Shimogamo Shrine. During this festival, people wade through a shallow stream within the shrine grounds to cleanse themselves and pray for good health and well-being. It is believed that passing through the water helps purify the soul and ward off evil spirits.

Natural Setting

Shimogamo Shrine is located along the banks of the Kamo River and is surrounded by lush greenery and trees. The shrine's picturesque setting provides a serene and refreshing environment for visitors to enjoy while exploring the sacred grounds.

Spiritual Practices

Shimogamo Shrine offers various spiritual practices and rituals for visitors to partake in, such as making offerings, praying for good fortune, and seeking blessings. The shrine serves as a place of worship and reflection, allowing individuals to connect with the divine and seek spiritual guidance.

HIDDEN GEMS

On the island of Honshu is the metropolis of Kyoto, which was once the capitol of Japan. It is well-known for its many classical Buddhist monasteries, as well as for its parks, royal residences, Shinto shrines, and traditional wooden homes. It is also well-known for its formal customs, including geisha, female performers frequently seen in the Gion neighborhood, and kaiseki dining, which consists of multiple plates of exact foods. Here are the best places to visit in Kyoto:

Kinkakuji

The lovely Golden Pavilion is the main attraction at Kinkakuji, a Buddhist shrine in northern Kyoto. But you ought to also saunter through its Japanese landscape. A pond that mirrors the gilded pavilion in this park demonstrates the fusion of natural and man-made design. Also designed into the scenery is a representation of well-known locations in Japanese writing. It is built on the simple landscape designs of the Muromachi era.

Nijo Castle

The ramparts, towers, and moat of Nijo Castle are all in excellent condition. The compound, which consists of several buildings and numerous significant works of art, is well-known for being the location where the emperor decided to issue the edict that brought an end to the country's once-dominant Shogunate. Highlighted are the East Gate (Higashi Otemon, the castle's main entrance) and the Inner Gate (Karamon), which is famous for its fine carvings and ornamental metalwork. The ornate Mikuruma-yose is another must-see in addition to this. It's enjoyable to stroll through the castle's lovely grounds.

Kyoto Imperial Palace

The Kyoto Imperial Palace, also known as the Kyoto Gosho, is a historic and culturally significant landmark located in Kyoto, Japan. It was once the residence of the Emperor of Japan until the Imperial Family moved to Tokyo in 1868. The palace is now used for official ceremonies and events, preserving its historical and symbolic importance.

The Kyoto Imperial Palace is situated in the heart of Kyoto within the Kyoto Imperial Park, a large green space that provides a tranquil escape from the bustling city. The palace complex consists of several buildings, including the Shishinden (Ceremonial Hall), the Seiryoden (the former Emperor's living quarters), and the Kogosho (the former Empress's living quarters).

Visitors to the Kyoto Imperial Palace can explore the grounds and some of the buildings on guided tours led by the Imperial Household Agency. These tours offer insight into the architecture, history, and traditions of the Japanese Imperial Family. It's essential to check the tour schedule and make a reservation in advance, as the number of visitors allowed per day is limited to preserve the site.

The palace's architecture showcases traditional Japanese design, including the use of wooden structures and elegantly crafted gardens. It's a remarkable place to learn about Japan's imperial history and appreciate the cultural heritage that Kyoto represents.

When visiting the Kyoto Imperial Palace, remember to show respect for the site's cultural significance and follow any guidelines provided by the Imperial Household Agency or the staff during your tour.

Kyoto's Bamboo Forest

The Kyoto Bamboo Forest, also known as the Arashiyama Bamboo Grove, is one of Kyoto's most iconic and enchanting natural attractions. Located in the Arashiyama district on the western outskirts of Kyoto, the Bamboo Forest is a serene and magical place that captivates visitors with its towering bamboo stalks and tranquil ambiance. Key features of the Kyoto Bamboo Forest include:

Towering Bamboo Stalks

The forest is characterized by an extensive network of tall bamboo stalks that create a unique canopy overhead. The bamboo shoots skyward, forming a tunnel-like pathway that envelops visitors in a surreal and peaceful environment.

Walking Path

A well-maintained walking path winds through the Bamboo Forest, allowing visitors to stroll amidst the bamboo groves. The path is relatively short, making it accessible for people of all ages.

Sound of Rustling Bamboo

As the wind gently blows through the bamboo grove, the stalks sway and create a calming rustling sound, adding to the tranquil atmosphere.

Kodai-ji Temple

The Bamboo Forest is located close to Kodai-ji Temple, a beautiful Zen Buddhist temple that you can visit during your time in the area.

The Bamboo Forest is especially stunning during the early morning or late afternoon when the light filters through the bamboo, creating mesmerizing patterns and shadows. It is a popular destination for tourists and locals alike, so visiting during weekdays or early mornings can provide a more peaceful experience.

The Arashiyama district offers more than just the Bamboo Forest. Visitors can also explore the nearby Tenryu-ji Temple, the Togetsukyo Bridge over the Hozu River, and the charming streets of Arashiyama with its traditional shops and eateries.

Remember to be respectful when visiting the Bamboo Forest, as it is not only a tourist attraction but also a place of natural beauty and serenity. Admire the surroundings, take photos, but avoid touching or damaging the bamboo, and keep noise levels low to preserve the tranquility of this remarkable natural wonder in Kyoto.

Philosopher's Path

The Philosopher's Path, also known as Tetsugaku no Michi in Japanese, is a picturesque walking trail in Kyoto, Japan. This serene pathway follows a cherry tree-lined canal, offering a tranquil and scenic route that is particularly popular during the cherry blossom season. Key features of the Philosopher's Path include:

Cherry Blossoms

One of the main attractions of the Philosopher's Path is the beautiful cherry blossom trees that line the canal. During the spring, usually in early April, the path becomes a breathtaking tunnel of pink and white cherry blossoms, creating a magical atmosphere for visitors.

Scenic Views

The walking trail meanders through residential neighborhoods and small temples, providing scenic views of traditional Kyoto architecture, well-tended gardens, and glimpses of local life.

Honen-in Temple

Along the Philosopher's Path, you'll find Honen-in Temple, a serene and quiet temple known for its beautiful garden and tranquil atmosphere.

Eikan-do Zenrin-ji Temple

This temple is located close to the northern end of the Philosopher's Path and is renowned for its stunning autumn foliage during the fall season.

The Philosopher's Path is named after the influential Japanese philosopher Nishida Kitaro, who was said to use this path for daily meditation during his time as a professor at Kyoto University.

The path is approximately two kilometers long and can be comfortably covered on foot in about 30 minutes to an hour, depending on your pace and how much time you spend exploring the surroundings. It is a pleasant and peaceful walk, making it an ideal escape from the hustle and bustle of the city.

Whether you visit during the cherry blossom season, enjoy the vibrant autumn foliage, or explore the path during other times of the year, the Philosopher's Path offers a serene and contemplative experience in one of Kyoto's most charming neighborhoods.

Kyoto Aquarium

Kyoto Aquarium, also known as Kyoto Aquarium Umekoji Park, is a modern and family-friendly attraction located in Kyoto, Japan. It is situated in Umekoji Park, which is within walking distance from Kyoto Station, making it easily accessible for tourists and locals alike. Key features of Kyoto Aquarium include:

Marine Life Exhibits

The aquarium houses various exhibits showcasing marine life from different parts of the world. Visitors can explore colorful coral reefs, watch playful dolphins, and see various fish species up close.

Penguin Parade

One of the highlights of the aquarium is the penguin parade, where visitors can watch adorable penguins march and play around the designated area.

Giant Salamander Tank

Kyoto Aquarium is known for its large tank dedicated to the Japanese giant salamander, one of the world's largest amphibians.

Interactive Zones

The aquarium offers interactive zones where visitors can touch and interact with some marine creatures, providing an engaging and educational experience.

Jellyfish Tunnel

The aquarium features a mesmerizing jellyfish tunnel, where visitors can immerse themselves in a captivating display of floating and glowing jellyfish.

Shows and Presentations

Throughout the day, the aquarium hosts various shows and presentations, including dolphin shows and feeding demonstrations.

Ohara

Ohara is a scenic rural village located in the mountains of northern Kyoto, Japan. It is known for its peaceful and nostalgic atmosphere, picturesque landscapes, and historical temples. Here's more information about Ohara:

Natural Beauty

Ohara is surrounded by beautiful countryside, lush green mountains, and pristine forests. The village offers a refreshing escape from the city, with its serene and tranquil environment. It is particularly famous for its natural scenery during the spring cherry blossom season and the autumn foliage season when the vibrant colors of the leaves create a stunning backdrop.

Temples and Gardens

Ohara is home to several historic temples and gardens that showcase the rich cultural heritage of the area. Sanzen-in Temple is one of the main attractions, known for its tranquil gardens, moss-covered statues, and picturesque ponds. Jakkoin Temple is another notable temple, featuring beautiful gardens and panoramic views of the surrounding mountains.

Otonashi Waterfall

Otonashi Waterfall is a hidden gem located near Ohara. It is a small, peaceful waterfall surrounded by moss-covered rocks and lush vegetation. The tranquil setting provides a perfect spot for relaxation and contemplation.

Farming Community

Ohara is an agricultural village known for its traditional farming practices. Visitors can experience the rural lifestyle and learn about local agricultural traditions by visiting local farms or participating in hands-on activities such as harvesting seasonal crops or making traditional food products.

Local Cuisine

Ohara is renowned for its fresh and delicious local produce. Many restaurants and cafes in the area serve traditional Japanese dishes made from locally sourced ingredients. One of the popular local specialties is "Ohara Sansai," a dish made with various wild mountain vegetables.

Shorin-an

Shorin-an is a peaceful and secluded tea house located in Ohara. It offers a serene environment for tea ceremonies and provides visitors with an opportunity to experience the art of tea and learn about Japanese tea culture.

Hiking and Nature Trails

Ohara is surrounded by scenic hiking trails that allow visitors to explore the natural beauty of the area. The trails lead to picturesque viewpoints, hidden temples, and waterfalls, offering a chance to connect with nature and enjoy outdoor activities.

Kurama

Kurama is a quaint and picturesque village located in the mountains to the north of Kyoto. Known for its natural beauty, historic sites, and spiritual significance, Kurama offers a serene and unique experience for visitors. Here's more information about Kurama:

Kurama-dera Temple

Kurama-dera is a Buddhist temple situated on Mount Kurama. Founded over 1,000 years ago, the temple holds great historical and spiritual significance. The temple features stunning architecture, serene gardens, and panoramic views of the surrounding area. It is also known for its Tengu statues, mythical creatures in Japanese folklore.

Kurama Onsen

Kurama is famous for its hot springs, and the Kurama Onsen is a popular destination for relaxation and rejuvenation. Nestled in the tranquil mountains, the onsen offers indoor and outdoor baths where visitors can soak in the therapeutic waters while enjoying the scenic beauty of the surrounding nature.

Kurama-Kibune Trail

The Kurama-Kibune Trail is a scenic hiking trail that connects Kurama with the neighboring village of Kibune. The trail takes you through lush forests, along mountain streams, and past scenic viewpoints. It offers an opportunity to immerse yourself in nature and enjoy the serene beauty of the mountains.

Fire Festival

Kurama hosts an annual Fire Festival, known as Kurama no Hi Matsuri, on October 22nd. The festival features large torches carried through the streets and a spectacular display of fire on the mountainside. It is a unique and vibrant event that attracts many visitors.

Kurama-dera Kurama Fire Festival

In addition to the main Fire Festival, Kurama-dera Temple holds its own Kurama Fire Festival on the same day as the village's festival. The temple is beautifully illuminated, and visitors can witness the procession of portable shrines, performances, and fireworks, creating a magical and festive atmosphere.

Nature and Scenic Views

Kurama is surrounded by natural beauty, with lush forests, peaceful streams, and breathtaking views of the mountains. The area is particularly captivating during the cherry blossom season in spring and the autumn foliage season when the vibrant colors of the leaves create a stunning backdrop.

Spiritual Retreat

Kurama is considered a spiritual retreat where visitors can find peace and tranquility. Many people come to Kurama to escape the bustling city and immerse themselves in the serene and serene environment of the mountains.

Kibune

Kibune is a charming village located in the mountains to the north of Kyoto. Known for its natural beauty, spiritual sites, and unique dining experience, Kibune offers a peaceful and picturesque getaway from the city. Here's more information about Kibune:

Kifune Shrine

Kibune is home to Kifune Shrine, a Shinto shrine dedicated to the god of water. The shrine is nestled in a forested area and is known for its striking red color and beautiful setting along the Kibune River. Visitors can explore the shrine's various buildings, participate in water-related rituals, and enjoy the serene atmosphere.

Dining Over the River

Kibune is famous for its unique dining experience known as "kawadoko." In the summer months, restaurants build platforms called "yuka" over the Kibune River. Visitors can enjoy traditional Kyoto cuisine while sitting above the flowing water, creating a delightful and refreshing dining experience.

Kurama-Kibune Trail

The Kurama-Kibune Trail is a scenic hiking trail that connects Kibune with the neighboring village of Kurama. The trail takes you through lush forests, past peaceful streams, and offers breathtaking views of the mountains. It's a great opportunity to immerse yourself in nature and enjoy the tranquility of the surroundings.

Summer Illuminations

During the summer months, Kibune holds evening illuminations along the Kibune River. The area is beautifully lit up, creating a magical and romantic atmosphere. It's a lovely time to visit and enjoy the enchanting ambiance.

Nature and Scenic Beauty

Kibune is surrounded by pristine nature, with dense forests, clear streams, and picturesque landscapes. The area is particularly stunning during the spring cherry blossom season and the autumn foliage season when the colors of nature come alive.

Ryokan Experience

Kibune is known for its traditional Japanese inns, called ryokans. Staying at a ryokan in Kibune allows you to immerse yourself in Japanese hospitality and experience the traditional way of life. Many ryokans offer hot spring baths, kaiseki meals, and serene surroundings.

Outdoor Activities

Kibune's natural surroundings provide opportunities for outdoor activities such as hiking, nature walks, and birdwatching. The tranquil environment and beautiful scenery make it an ideal destination for those seeking a peaceful and rejuvenating outdoor experience.

KYOTO ONSENS

Kyoto, known for its rich cultural heritage, is not as famous for onsen (hot spring) resorts as other regions in Japan. However, there are still a few onsen options in and around Kyoto that offer a relaxing and rejuvenating experience. Here are some onsen options in and near Kyoto:

Funaoka Onsen

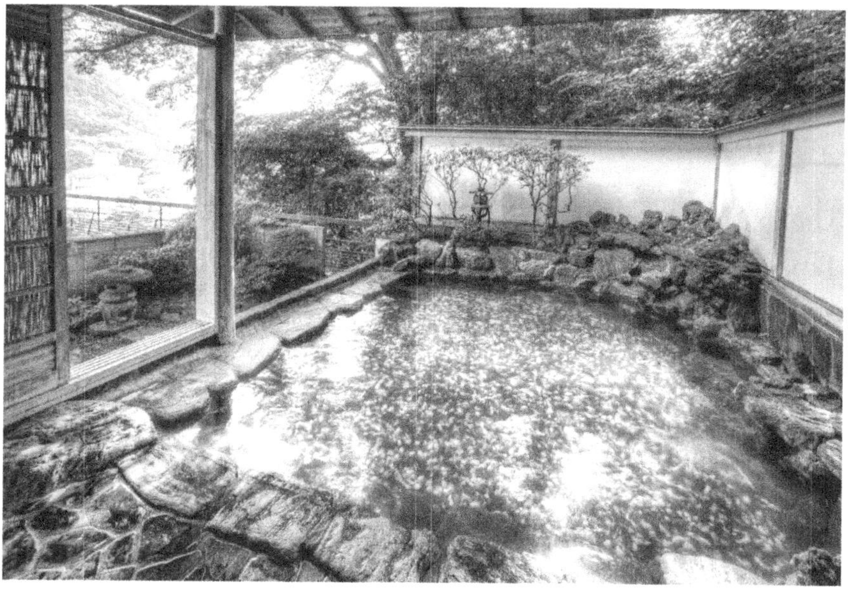

Funaoka Onsen is one of Kyoto's oldest and most well-known public bathhouses. It offers a traditional Japanese onsen experience and is a popular choice for both locals and visitors seeking relaxation and rejuvenation. Here's what you can expect when visiting Funaoka Onsen:

History

Funaoka Onsen has a long history dating back over 100 years. It has been serving the local community and travelers for generations, making it an integral part of Kyoto's cultural heritage.

Location

Funaoka Onsen is located in the Kita Ward of Kyoto, making it easily accessible from various parts of the city. It is not far from popular tourist areas like Kinkaku-ji (Golden Pavilion) and Daitoku-ji Temple.

Architecture and Atmosphere

The bathhouse retains its traditional charm with a classic Japanese wooden structure. Upon entering, you'll find a cozy and nostalgic ambiance that reflects the history and character of the onsen.

Gender-Separated Baths

Like most traditional onsen, Funaoka Onsen offers separate bathing areas for men and women. The baths are spacious and feature indoor and outdoor bathing options.

Hot Spring Waters

Funaoka Onsen's waters are sourced from natural hot springs, and the mineral-rich properties are believed to have various health benefits. The hot spring waters are typically kept at a comfortable temperature, making them ideal for a relaxing soak.

Rotenburo (Outdoor Bath)

Funaoka Onsen has a lovely outdoor bath, known as a rotenburo, where you can bathe while enjoying the fresh air and natural surroundings. The rotenburo experience is especially enjoyable during different seasons when the garden may showcase seasonal blooms or colors.

Tattoo-Friendly

Unlike some onsen establishments that have strict policies against tattoos due to historical associations with organized crime, Funaoka Onsen allows visitors with tattoos to enjoy the baths.

Festive Atmosphere

Funaoka Onsen has a lively atmosphere, especially during festivals and special events. These occasions provide a chance to experience the onsen with additional festivities and cultural performances.

Community Space

The bathhouse serves as a social space for the local community, offering an opportunity to connect with Kyoto residents and experience an essential aspect of Japanese culture.

Kurama Onsen

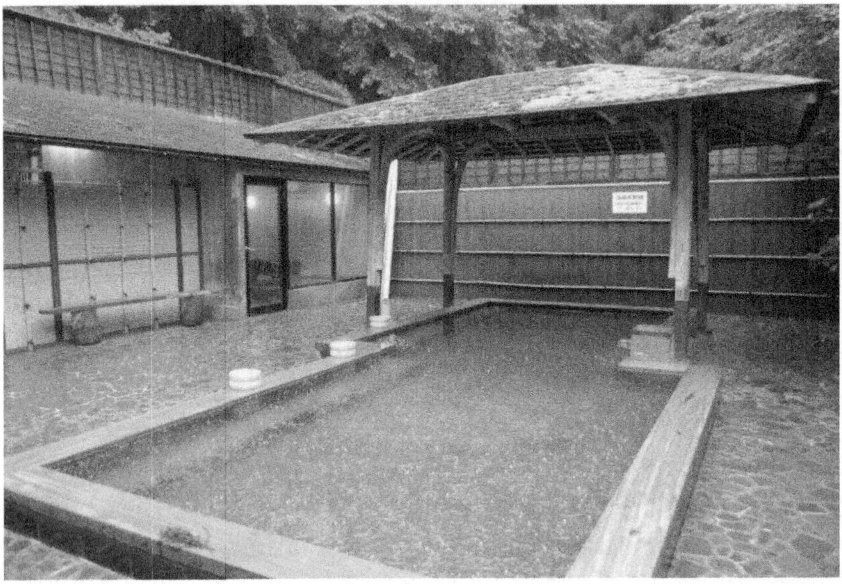

Kurama Onsen is a charming hot spring resort located in the mountainous village of Kurama, which is just north of Kyoto, Japan. This onsen offers visitors a unique and serene experience, making it a popular getaway from the bustling city of Kyoto. Here's what you can expect when visiting Kurama Onsen:

Scenic Location

Kurama Onsen is situated amidst a peaceful and picturesque setting in the Kurama Mountains. The natural beauty of the surrounding forests and mountains provides a tranquil atmosphere that complements the relaxing onsen experience.

Access

To reach Kurama Onsen, you can take a scenic train ride from Kyoto Station to Kurama Station. From there, it's a short walk through the charming village to the onsen. The journey itself is part of the experience, as the train ride offers glimpses of rural landscapes.

Outdoor and Indoor Baths

Kurama Onsen offers both indoor and outdoor baths. The outdoor baths, known as rotenburo, allow you to immerse yourself in the soothing hot spring waters while enjoying the natural beauty of the surroundings.

Mineral-Rich Waters

The hot spring waters at Kurama Onsen are said to be rich in minerals, which are believed to have therapeutic benefits for the skin and body. Many visitors find the experience of soaking in these mineral-rich waters to be incredibly rejuvenating.

Mixed-Bathing Option

Kurama Onsen is one of the few places in Kyoto that offers mixed-gender bathing in specific outdoor baths during certain hours. This can be a unique experience for those interested in traditional Japanese onsen culture.

Hiking Opportunities

Beyond the onsen, Kurama is known for its hiking trails and the famous Kurama-dera Temple. Visitors can take a short hike through the forested trail to reach the temple, which offers breathtaking views of the valley.

Seasonal Beauty

Kurama Onsen is beautiful year-round, and each season brings its own unique charm. During autumn, the surrounding mountains and forests are adorned with vibrant autumn foliage, making it a popular time to visit.

Traditional Ryokan Experience

Kurama Onsen is housed in a traditional ryokan (Japanese inn), offering an authentic Japanese experience. Staying at the ryokan allows guests to fully immerse themselves in the onsen culture and hospitality.

Arashiyama Onsen

During my trip to Japan a couple of years ago, I had the wonderful opportunity to visit Arashiyama Onsen in Kyoto. As a fan of traditional Japanese culture and hot springs, I was really looking forward to this experience.

My journey to the Arashiyama district was nothing short of enchanting. The area was rich with lush greenery and dotted with traditional wooden buildings, giving it a charming and picturesque ambiance. When I arrived at the ryokan, I was greeted by the friendly staff who made me feel instantly welcome.

The moment I stepped into Arashiyama Onsen, I was captivated by its peaceful and serene atmosphere. The ryokan had an elegant, old-world charm, and the soothing sound of water flowing in the garden added to the sense of tranquility. The traditional Japanese decor and tatami flooring further immersed me in the cultural experience.

After completing the check-in process, I eagerly made my way to the open-air bath. The beauty of the garden that lay before me was breathtaking. Cherry blossom trees swayed gently in the breeze, and the view was like something out of a postcard. I couldn't wait to immerse myself in the natural hot spring water while enjoying the picturesque surroundings.

As I dipped into the open-air bath, the warm water enveloped me, easing away any tension I had been carrying from my travels. The hot springs were incredibly rejuvenating, and I could feel my worries melting away with each passing minute. The experience of soaking in the onsen while admiring the beauty of the garden was truly magical. Time seemed to slow down, and I felt a deep sense of relaxation and connection with nature.

I spent a considerable amount of time in the onsen, indulging in this blissful escape. Afterward, I wrapped myself in a comfortable yukata provided by the ryokan and headed to the dining area for a traditional kaiseki meal. The delicately prepared dishes featured seasonal ingredients and were a true gastronomic delight.

Staying at Arashiyama Onsen was more than just a luxurious experience; it was a journey into the heart of Japanese culture and hospitality. The warm smiles of the staff, the breathtaking surroundings, and the serene atmosphere left an indelible mark on my soul. It was a memory I will cherish for a lifetime, and I left Kyoto with a deep appreciation for the beauty and tranquility that the Arashiyama district and its onsen had to offer.

Rakuhoku Onsen

Rakuhoku Onsen is located in the northern part of Kyoto and offers a peaceful and tranquil atmosphere. The area is well-known for its natural hot springs, and there are several onsen facilities in the region.

Kameoka Onsen

Kameoka Onsen, also known as Kameoka City Onsen, is a popular hot spring resort located in Kameoka City, which is in the western part of Kyoto Prefecture, Japan. Kameoka is not far from Kyoto City and is accessible by train or bus, making it a convenient destination for a day trip or a short getaway from Kyoto. Here are some key features of Kameoka Onsen:

Hot Spring Facilities

Kameoka Onsen offers various onsen facilities, including ryokans (traditional Japanese inns) and public bathhouses. These facilities provide a range of bathing options, including indoor and outdoor baths with mineral-rich hot spring waters.

Mineral-Rich Waters

The hot spring waters in Kameoka are known for their mineral content and therapeutic properties. Bathing in these natural hot springs is believed to have various health benefits, including relaxation and rejuvenation.

Scenic Surroundings

Kameoka is surrounded by beautiful natural landscapes, including mountains and rivers. Some onsen facilities may offer outdoor baths with views of the scenic surroundings, allowing guests to soak in the hot springs while enjoying the peaceful environment.

Ryokan Experience

Staying in a ryokan in Kameoka Onsen provides an authentic Japanese experience. Ryokans typically offer traditional tatami-floored rooms, futon bedding, and kaiseki (multi-course) meals featuring local and seasonal ingredients.

Community and Cultural Events

Kameoka Onsen may host various community and cultural events throughout the year, providing visitors with opportunities to engage in local traditions and festivities.

Proximity to Kyoto

Kameoka Onsen's accessibility from Kyoto City makes it a convenient destination for tourists and locals looking to experience hot spring baths without venturing too far from the urban center.

Kyoto Prefecture Onsen Resorts

Kyoto Prefecture is not as well-known for its onsen resorts compared to other regions in Japan. However, there are still some onsen facilities and resorts scattered throughout the prefecture, offering a relaxing and rejuvenating experience. While not directly in Kyoto City, these onsen resorts are accessible within a reasonable distance from the city and provide a chance to experience the hot spring culture of the region. Here are some onsen resorts in and around Kyoto Prefecture:

Arima Onsen (Hyogo Prefecture)

Arima Onsen is one of the oldest and most famous hot spring resorts in Japan. Located in the neighboring Hyogo Prefecture, it is easily accessible from Kyoto City. Arima Onsen offers both "gold" and "silver" hot spring waters, each with different mineral properties, and is known for its therapeutic benefits.

Kinosaki Onsen (Hyogo Prefecture)

Kinosaki Onsen is another well-known hot spring town in Hyogo Prefecture. It features seven public bathhouses, each with its unique charm, and visitors can enjoy strolling through the charming streets while wearing traditional yukata robes.

Shirahama Onsen (Wakayama Prefecture)

Shirahama Onsen is located in Wakayama Prefecture, and it is known for its hot spring baths with views of the Pacific Ocean. The area also offers beautiful beaches, making it an ideal destination for those seeking both onsen relaxation and coastal beauty.

Kurama Onsen (Kyoto Prefecture)

Kurama Onsen is located in the mountainous village of Kurama, just north of Kyoto. It is accessible by train and a short hike through a beautiful forested trail. Kurama Onsen provides a unique and serene onsen experience with mineral-rich hot spring waters.

KYOTO GARDENS AND PARKS

Kyoto is renowned for its stunning gardens and parks, which reflect the city's deep appreciation for nature and the art of landscaping. Here are some of the notable gardens and parks in Kyoto:

Arashiyama Monkey Park

The Arashiyama Monkey Park, also known as Iwatayama Monkey Park, is a popular tourist attraction located in the

Arashiyama district of Kyoto, Japan. This park is renowned for its troop of Japanese macaque monkeys, also known as snow monkeys, which visitors can observe in a semi-wild environment. Key features of the Arashiyama Monkey Park include:

Observation Deck

The main highlight of the Monkey Park is its observation deck located at the top of Mt. Iwatayama. To reach the observation deck, visitors need to hike up a mountain trail that takes about 20 to 30 minutes. The hike itself offers scenic views of the surrounding area, including the Hozu River and the city of Kyoto.

Monkey Interaction

At the observation deck, visitors can encounter a troop of Japanese macaque monkeys that roam freely within the designated area. The monkeys are used to human presence and are not aggressive, but it's important to follow the park's rules to ensure the safety of both visitors and the animals.

Feeding the Monkeys

Visitors can purchase food (special monkey food pellets) at the entrance and feed the monkeys from inside the designated feeding area on the observation deck. Feeding the monkeys provides a unique and memorable experience for visitors.

Educational Exhibits

The park also offers educational exhibits about the behavior and ecology of Japanese macaque monkeys, providing insights into their social structure and interactions.

Kinkaku-ji (Golden Pavilion) Garden

The Kinkaku-ji (Golden Pavilion) Garden is an exquisite and meticulously designed landscape surrounding the famous Zen Buddhist temple in Kyoto, Japan. The garden complements the splendor of the Golden Pavilion and plays a crucial role in enhancing the temple's serene and captivating ambiance. It is a prime example of Japanese garden design, incorporating natural elements and carefully arranged features to create a harmonious and visually stunning environment. Here are some key features and highlights of the Kinkaku-ji Garden:

Reflecting Pond

The garden features a large pond, known as Kyoko-chi, which serves as a reflecting pool for the Golden Pavilion. The mirror-like surface of the pond beautifully captures the image of the gilded temple, creating a breathtaking sight that appears almost surreal.

Islands and Stones

The pond contains small islands and strategically placed stones, each with its symbolic meaning. The islands represent mythological islands from Buddhist and Taoist beliefs, while the stones are carefully positioned to evoke a sense of balance and harmony.

Vegetation and Trees

The garden is meticulously landscaped with a variety of trees and plants, carefully chosen for their seasonal beauty. Cherry trees bloom in spring, while maple trees display vibrant colors in autumn, enhancing the garden's beauty throughout the year.

Walking Paths and Bridges

Meandering paths and wooden bridges lead visitors through the garden, allowing them to enjoy different perspectives of the Golden Pavilion and its surroundings. The walking paths are designed to encourage contemplation and a sense of tranquility.

Tea Garden

Adjacent to the main garden, there is a small tea garden called Sekka-tei. This traditional tea house and garden offer visitors the opportunity to experience a traditional Japanese tea ceremony while enjoying the view of Kinkaku-ji and its reflection in the pond.

Seasonal Beauty

The Kinkaku-ji Garden transforms with the changing seasons, offering visitors a unique experience throughout the year. In spring, cherry blossoms create a picturesque scene, while autumn foliage bathes the garden in vibrant colors.

Cultural Significance

The Kinkaku-ji Garden, together with the Golden Pavilion, has been designated as a UNESCO World Heritage Site, recognizing its cultural and historical importance as a symbol of Japan's rich cultural heritage.

Katsura Imperial Villa and Garden

The Katsura Imperial Villa (Katsura Rikyū) and its garden, located in Kyoto, Japan, are considered masterpieces of Japanese traditional architecture and landscape design. The villa was originally built as a private residence for the Hachijo-no-miya imperial family during the Edo period (17th century) and later became an imperial villa. Today, it is one of the most important cultural and historical sites in Japan, attracting visitors with its exquisite architectural features and meticulously crafted gardens.

Architectural Design

The Katsura Imperial Villa is renowned for its elegant and refined architectural style, representing the pinnacle of Japanese traditional architecture. The design of the villa showcases the principles of wabi-sabi, emphasizing simplicity, asymmetry, and the appreciation of natural materials. The buildings are constructed of wood and feature traditional elements such as tatami mat flooring, sliding doors (fusuma), and beautiful interior and exterior views.

Garden Design

The gardens of the Katsura Imperial Villa are equally stunning and are considered a masterpiece of Japanese landscape design. The gardens combine natural beauty with carefully planned elements to create a harmonious and serene atmosphere. The garden incorporates a large central pond surrounded by carefully positioned rocks, trees, and shrubs. Stone pathways, bridges, and stepping stones lead visitors through the landscape, encouraging a contemplative and meditative experience.

Tea Houses

Within the villa's gardens, you'll find several tea houses that exemplify the principles of the traditional Japanese tea ceremony. These tea houses offer visitors an opportunity to immerse themselves in the art of tea and the philosophy of simplicity and mindfulness.

Imperial Cultural Heritage

As an imperial property, the Katsura Imperial Villa is considered an essential part of Japan's cultural heritage. The villa and garden have been meticulously preserved over the centuries, and their beauty and historical significance have been recognized both nationally and internationally.

Visitor Access

Access to the Katsura Imperial Villa is restricted, and visitors are required to book guided tours in advance through the Imperial Household Agency. The tours are conducted in Japanese, and a limited number of international tours with English-speaking guides are available on specific dates.

Ryoan-ji Temple and Zen Garden

Ryoan-ji Temple is a historic Zen Buddhist temple located in Kyoto, Japan, known for its minimalist and iconic Zen rock garden. The temple and its garden are considered masterpieces of Japanese Zen culture and have been designated as a UNESCO World Heritage Site. Ryoan-ji is a popular destination for visitors seeking a contemplative and tranquil experience, as the Zen garden is particularly renowned for its simplicity and enigmatic design.

History and Architecture

Ryoan-ji Temple was originally established in the late 15th century as a villa for a powerful aristocratic family. Later, it was converted into a Zen temple, and its current form dates back to the 17th century. The temple's main building, called Hojo, features traditional Japanese architecture with tatami mat flooring and sliding doors, providing a serene setting for meditation and contemplation.

Zen Rock Garden

The Zen rock garden at Ryoan-ji is one of the most famous and enigmatic in the world. It is a dry garden, known as a karesansui, composed of carefully raked white gravel and fifteen large rocks strategically placed on the ground. The rocks are arranged in such a way that, from any vantage point, it is impossible to see all fifteen rocks simultaneously. This arrangement is believed to provoke a meditative state and encourage self-reflection, as the viewer is encouraged to contemplate the garden and its design.

Simplicity and Symbolism

The simplicity of the Zen rock garden at Ryoan-ji is a key aspect of its design philosophy. The white gravel represents water, while the rocks symbolize islands or mountains rising from the sea. The sparse composition encourages visitors to focus on the natural elements and encourages a sense of tranquility and inner peace.

Seasonal Beauty

Ryoan-ji's beauty changes with the seasons, offering visitors a different experience throughout the year. In spring, cherry blossoms adorn the temple grounds, while autumn brings a stunning display of colorful foliage, enhancing the contemplative atmosphere of the Zen garden.

Tea House and Pond Garden

Adjacent to the Zen rock garden, Ryoan-ji also features a traditional tea house and a pond garden called Kyoyochi. The tea house provides visitors with an opportunity to experience a traditional Japanese tea ceremony in a serene setting. The pond garden complements the Zen garden, adding another layer of natural beauty to the temple complex.

Cultural Significance

Ryoan-ji Temple and its Zen rock garden are significant cultural assets in Japan and have a profound influence on Japanese aesthetics and philosophy. Many visitors come to Ryoan-ji seeking a moment of contemplation and spiritual reflection amidst the serenity of the garden.

Tofuku-ji Temple and Gardens

Tofuku-ji is a historic Zen Buddhist temple located in Kyoto, Japan. It is one of the five great Zen temples of Kyoto and is renowned for its beautiful gardens and impressive architecture. The temple complex offers visitors a glimpse into Japan's Zen Buddhist tradition, as well as the opportunity to immerse themselves in the serenity of its carefully landscaped gardens. Here are some key features and highlights of Tofuku-ji Temple and Gardens:

History and Architecture

Tofuku-ji Temple was founded in 1236 during the Kamakura period and holds great historical and cultural significance. The temple features a classic Zen architectural style, with simple and elegant wooden structures that exemplify the Zen aesthetic of modesty and tranquility.

Hojo Garden

The Hojo Garden, located within the temple complex, is one of Tofuku-ji's main attractions. It is a traditional Zen garden known for its minimalist design, which emphasizes the beauty of simplicity and natural elements. The garden features carefully raked white gravel, symbolizing water, with meticulously placed rocks and islands that represent mountains rising from the sea.

Tsutenkyo Bridge and Maple Trees

The Tsutenkyo Bridge is another notable feature of Tofuku-ji. This wooden bridge spans across a valley, offering breathtaking views of the surrounding maple trees. The temple is particularly famous for its vibrant autumn foliage, attracting numerous visitors who come to witness the stunning red and golden hues of the maple leaves.

Valley of Maple Trees

The valley surrounding the Tsutenkyo Bridge is aptly named the Valley of Maple Trees. During the autumn season, the valley becomes a vibrant tapestry of colors, making it a popular spot for photographers and nature enthusiasts.

Sanmon Gate

The Sanmon Gate is Tofuku-ji's main gate and is one of the oldest wooden gates in Japan. It is an impressive three-story structure that adds to the temple's historical and architectural significance.

Zen Meditation and Practice

Tofuku-ji is an active Zen temple, and visitors have the opportunity to experience Zen meditation and participate in Buddhist rituals. The temple's serene atmosphere makes it an ideal place for contemplation and spiritual reflection.

Cultural Significance

Tofuku-ji Temple and Gardens are designated as National Historic Sites and are also part of the Historic Monuments of Ancient Kyoto, a UNESCO World Heritage Site, highlighting their cultural importance and value.

Seasonal Beauty

While the autumn foliage is a prime attraction, Tofuku-ji's gardens offer a different charm throughout the year. In spring, cherry blossoms bloom, and in summer, the lush greenery creates a peaceful environment for visitors to enjoy.

Maruyama Park

Maruyama Park is a beautiful and popular public park located in the Higashiyama district of Kyoto, Japan. It is one of the city's most cherished and picturesque parks, attracting both locals and tourists throughout the year. Maruyama Park is known for its scenic beauty, seasonal attractions, and historical significance, making it a delightful destination for nature lovers and culture enthusiasts alike.

Cherry Blossoms (Sakura)

One of the main highlights of Maruyama Park is its stunning cherry blossom display during the spring season. When the cherry blossoms are in full bloom, usually around late March to early April, the park transforms into a sea of delicate pink and white flowers. This spectacle draws crowds of visitors who come to partake in traditional hanami (cherry blossom viewing) picnics under the blooming trees.

Weeping Cherry Tree (Shidarezakura)

The park is home to a magnificent weeping cherry tree, known as the Gion Shidarezakura, which is one of Kyoto's most famous cherry trees. When the weeping cherry tree blooms, it creates a breathtaking canopy of cascading cherry blossoms, adding to the park's enchanting ambiance.

Seasonal Beauty

While cherry blossom season is the park's most celebrated time, Maruyama Park's beauty extends throughout the year. In autumn, the park's maple trees transform into a fiery display of red and gold foliage, creating another enchanting scene for visitors to enjoy.

Pond and Tea House

Maruyama Park features a large pond called the Shoubutei Pond, surrounded by walking paths and lush greenery. There is also a traditional teahouse called Chashitsu Suirokaku, where visitors can experience a traditional Japanese tea ceremony while overlooking the pond and gardens.

Evening Illumination

During the cherry blossom season, Maruyama Park offers evening illuminations that bathe the cherry trees in soft light, creating a magical and romantic atmosphere. The illuminated cherry blossoms make the park a popular spot for nighttime strolls and photography.

Hanatouro Illumination Event

Maruyama Park is part of the Hanatouro illumination event that takes place in the Higashiyama district of Kyoto. The event features stunning light displays and lanterns that illuminate the park and nearby streets, creating a mesmerizing spectacle.

Historical Significance

Maruyama Park has a long history and has been a beloved destination for locals and travelers for centuries. It is said to have been established during the Heian period (794-1185), making it one of Kyoto's oldest public parks.

Kyoto Imperial Palace Park

The Kyoto Imperial Palace Park, also known as the Kyoto Gosho Park, is a serene and historically significant green space located in the heart of Kyoto, Japan. It surrounds the Kyoto Imperial Palace, which was once the residence of Japan's emperors. Today, while the palace itself is not open to the public except for special occasions and guided tours, the park offers visitors a chance to explore its tranquil gardens, enjoy picturesque scenery, and immerse themselves in Japan's rich imperial history.

Historical Significance

The Kyoto Imperial Palace has a long and storied history, dating back to the Heian period (794-1185). It was the residence of Japan's emperors until the capital was moved to Tokyo in 1869. The palace has seen numerous reconstructions over the centuries, and today's structures are faithful reproductions based on historical records.

Gardens and Scenery

The Kyoto Imperial Palace Park features meticulously landscaped gardens with traditional Japanese elements, including stone pathways, ponds, and carefully pruned trees. The park's design follows the principles of traditional Japanese garden aesthetics, creating a harmonious and peaceful environment for visitors to enjoy.

Cherry Blossoms (Sakura)

During the spring season, the park's cherry blossoms bloom, creating a captivating display of pink and white flowers. Cherry blossom viewing (hanami) is a popular activity in the park, attracting locals and tourists alike who come to celebrate the arrival of spring and witness the beauty of the cherry blossoms.

Autumn Foliage

In the autumn, the park's trees transform into a breathtaking array of red, orange, and gold hues. The vibrant autumn foliage adds to the park's charm and makes it an excellent spot for leisurely walks and photography.

Peaceful Atmosphere

The Kyoto Imperial Palace Park offers a peaceful and serene atmosphere, inviting visitors to take leisurely strolls and find respite from the bustling city. It is an ideal place for relaxation, reflection, and connecting with nature.

Guided Tours

While the interior of the Kyoto Imperial Palace is not open to the public without a reservation, guided tours are available for visitors to explore certain areas of the palace and learn about its historical and cultural significance.

Admission and Accessibility

Entrance to the Kyoto Imperial Palace Park is free, and it is open to the public year-round. The park is easily accessible by public transportation, making it a convenient destination for tourists exploring Kyoto's central area.

Zen Gardens

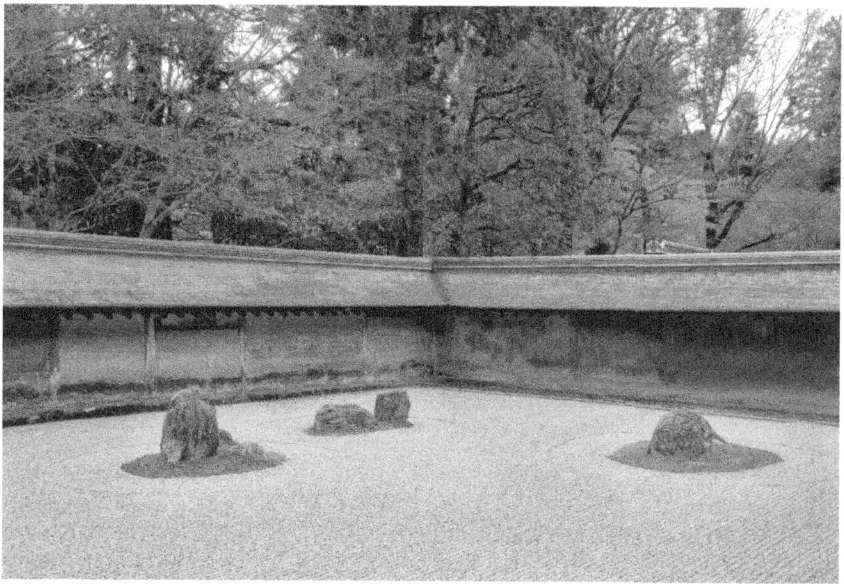

Zen gardens, also known as Japanese rock gardens or dry gardens, are iconic and meditative landscapes that originated in Japan. These gardens are designed to promote tranquility, contemplation, and a sense of inner peace. They are an essential element of Zen Buddhist temples and other traditional Japanese settings, showcasing the essence of simplicity, harmony, and nature.

Design and Elements

Zen gardens typically consist of carefully arranged rocks, gravel, sand, and sometimes moss. The design principles are based on minimalism and symbolism. Each element in the garden has a specific meaning, and the arrangement is thoughtfully planned to evoke natural landscapes such as mountains, islands, and seas.

Raked Patterns

One of the most recognizable features of Zen gardens is the raked patterns in the gravel or sand, known as karesansui. The patterns are often made to resemble ripples in water or waves, symbolizing the continuous flow of nature. Raking the patterns is also believed to be a form of meditation, helping practitioners to clear their minds and find inner calm.

Rocks

Rocks are a fundamental element in Zen gardens and are placed strategically to represent various features like mountains or islands. Larger rocks are often used to create focal points, while smaller rocks can symbolize islands in the sea.

Gravel or Sand

The use of gravel or sand in Zen gardens represents water or emptiness. The act of raking the gravel is meant to imitate the flow of water and create a sense of movement and tranquility.

Moss and Greenery

While not present in all Zen gardens, some incorporate moss and carefully pruned shrubs to add a touch of greenery and enhance the natural ambiance.

Contemplative Space

Zen gardens are intended to be contemplative spaces where visitors can meditate, find peace, and reflect on the impermanence of life and the harmony of nature.

Teahouse Gardens

Many teahouses in Japan have Zen gardens outside, where guests can relax and meditate before and after participating in the traditional Japanese tea ceremony.

Cultural Significance

Zen gardens have a profound cultural and spiritual significance in Japanese culture. They are seen as places of enlightenment and self-reflection, aligning with the principles of Zen Buddhism and its emphasis on mindfulness and living in the present moment.

Variations

While the classic Zen garden is the dry karesansui style, there are variations that incorporate water features like ponds or streams. These variations still maintain the principles of simplicity, balance, and natural symbolism.

Kyoto Botanical Garden

The Kyoto Botanical Garden, also known as Kyoto Prefectural Botanical Gardens, is a lush and enchanting green space located in Kyoto, Japan. It is one of the oldest and most significant botanical gardens in the country, offering visitors a diverse collection of plant species and a tranquil escape from the city's bustling streets. The garden serves as a haven for nature enthusiasts, researchers, and tourists alike, providing an opportunity to explore and appreciate the beauty and diversity of Japan's flora.

History

Established in 1924, the Kyoto Botanical Garden has a long history of plant conservation, research, and education. It is operated by the Kyoto Prefectural Government and is affiliated with Kyoto University.

Flora and Collections

The botanical garden boasts an extensive collection of plants, including a wide variety of Japanese and international species. Visitors can explore themed gardens, such as the Cherry Tree Garden, Iris Garden, and Rose Garden, showcasing seasonal blooms at their finest. There are also collections of native Japanese plants, traditional tea garden plants, and rare and endangered species.

Cherry Blossom Season

During the cherry blossom season in spring, the Kyoto Botanical Garden becomes a popular spot for hanami (cherry blossom viewing). Many varieties of cherry trees bloom in the garden, providing a stunning display of delicate pink and white flowers, attracting locals and tourists alike.

Conservatories

The botanical garden features several greenhouses and conservatories that house exotic plants from tropical and subtropical regions. These indoor spaces allow visitors to experience a wide range of plant life from different climates, regardless of the season.

Research and Conservation

The Kyoto Botanical Garden plays a vital role in plant research, conservation, and education. It serves as a center for studying Japan's flora, promoting biodiversity, and raising awareness about environmental conservation.

Educational Programs

The garden offers various educational programs and workshops for visitors of all ages, including guided tours, lectures, and hands-on activities related to botany and horticulture.

Scenic Walking Paths

Visitors can explore the garden's scenic walking paths, which meander through different landscapes and showcase a diverse range of plant species. The well-maintained paths provide a peaceful and relaxing environment for leisurely strolls and appreciation of nature.

Seasonal Beauty

The Kyoto Botanical Garden's charm changes with the seasons, offering different experiences throughout the year. From cherry blossoms in spring to colorful foliage in autumn, each season brings its unique beauty to the garden.

KYOTO MUSEUMS

Kyoto is home to a wide array of museums that showcase the city's rich history, culture, and artistic traditions. Here are some notable museums in Kyoto:

Kyoto National Museum

The Kyoto National Museum is one of Japan's most esteemed and significant museums, dedicated to preserving and showcasing the country's rich cultural heritage and artistic achievements. Located in Kyoto, the museum is situated in the Higashiyama district, close to several other notable cultural landmarks. It is a must-visit destination for those seeking to deepen their understanding of Japan's history, art, and traditional crafts.

History

The Kyoto National Museum was established in 1897 as the Imperial Household Museum, making it one of the oldest museums in Japan. Its initial purpose was to preserve and display art and artifacts from the imperial family's collection. Over time, the museum's focus expanded to encompass broader aspects of Japanese culture.

Collections

The museum's vast collection includes over 12,000 items, featuring a diverse range of cultural artifacts, fine arts, and traditional crafts. The exhibits encompass a broad historical timeline, from ancient to contemporary periods, providing visitors with a comprehensive view of Japan's artistic and cultural evolution.

Japanese Art and Crafts

The museum showcases traditional Japanese art forms, including ceramics, textiles, lacquerware, metalwork, and woodblock prints. Visitors can admire the intricate craftsmanship and artistic expressions that have been honed over centuries by skilled artisans.

Buddhist Art

The museum has a notable collection of Buddhist art, including sculptures, paintings, and other religious artifacts. These pieces offer insights into the development of Buddhism in Japan and its influence on the country's artistic traditions.

Special Exhibitions

In addition to its permanent collection, the Kyoto National Museum hosts special exhibitions that focus on specific themes or artists. These temporary exhibitions provide unique opportunities to see rare and exquisite items on loan from other institutions or private collections.

Cultural Events

The museum occasionally hosts cultural events, lectures, and workshops, providing visitors with a deeper understanding of the artworks and their historical contexts. These events offer engaging and educational experiences for museum-goers of all ages.

Tea House and Garden

Within the museum grounds, there is a traditional Japanese tea house and a serene garden. The tea house, named Seishoan, offers visitors the chance to experience an authentic Japanese tea ceremony, while the garden provides a peaceful oasis in the heart of the city.

Cultural and Historic Significance

The Kyoto National Museum is an integral part of Kyoto's cultural landscape and plays a vital role in preserving and promoting Japan's artistic and cultural heritage. It holds immense cultural and historic significance, reflecting the country's profound artistic achievements and traditions.

Kyoto Museum of Traditional Crafts

The Kyoto Museum of Traditional Crafts, also known as the Kyoto Traditional Crafts Center, is a fascinating museum dedicated to showcasing and preserving the traditional crafts of Kyoto, Japan. Located in the heart of Kyoto, the museum offers visitors a unique opportunity to learn about the city's rich craft heritage, witness artisans at work, and appreciate the exquisite craftsmanship that has been passed down through generations.

History and Purpose

The Kyoto Museum of Traditional Crafts was established in 1982 with the goal of promoting and preserving the traditional crafts of Kyoto. The museum serves as a hub for craftsmen to demonstrate their skills, and it aims to educate the public about the historical and cultural significance of traditional crafts in Japanese society.

Exhibits and Displays

The museum features an impressive array of traditional crafts from Kyoto, each representing the city's unique artistic traditions. Visitors can explore exhibits showcasing various crafts, including:

- **Kimono:** Displaying intricate kimono fabrics and designs, highlighting the artistry of Kyoto's textile industry.
- **Pottery:** Showcasing Kyoto's famous pottery styles, such as Kiyomizu ware and Raku ware, known for their elegance and beauty.
- **Metalwork:** Featuring exquisite metalwork objects, including tea ceremony utensils and ornate metal crafts.
- **Dolls and Toys:** Presenting traditional Kyoto dolls and traditional toys that hold cultural significance.
- **Traditional Woodworking:** Highlighting traditional woodworking techniques used in the creation of furniture and architectural elements.

Demonstrations and Workshops

One of the highlights of the Kyoto Museum of Traditional Crafts is the opportunity to witness live craft demonstrations. Skilled artisans regularly conduct live demonstrations, allowing visitors to see the intricate process of creating traditional crafts firsthand. Additionally, the museum offers workshops where visitors can participate in hands-on experiences and try their hand at some of the crafts under the guidance of experts.

Craft Shop

The museum has a craft shop where visitors can purchase authentic traditional crafts, including pottery, textiles, and other handcrafted items. It provides an opportunity to support local artisans and take home a unique and cherished souvenir.

Cultural and Historic Significance

The Kyoto Museum of Traditional Crafts plays a crucial role in preserving Japan's intangible cultural heritage and promoting the continuation of traditional craftsmanship. By showcasing these time-honored crafts, the museum fosters a deeper appreciation for the artistry, skills, and cultural values associated with traditional crafts.

Kyoto International Manga Museum

The Kyoto International Manga Museum is a unique and captivating destination for manga enthusiasts and visitors interested in Japanese pop culture. Located in Kyoto, Japan, the museum celebrates the art and history of manga, Japan's popular comic and graphic novel art form. It is a must-visit destination for manga lovers of all ages, providing a comprehensive and immersive experience into the world of manga.

History and Location

The Kyoto International Manga Museum was established in 2006 in a former elementary school building called Tatsuike Primary School. The location itself adds a touch of nostalgia and charm to the museum, as visitors can explore the classrooms and hallways that have been converted into manga reading rooms.

Vast Manga Collection

The museum houses an extensive collection of manga, ranging from vintage classics to contemporary works. There are thousands of manga titles available in different genres, themes, and styles. Visitors can freely browse and read the manga in multiple languages, providing an inclusive and enjoyable experience for both Japanese and international visitors.

Manga Exhibits and Displays

In addition to the vast manga collection, the museum features exhibits on the history of manga, influential manga artists, and the evolution of manga as an art form. These displays provide visitors with insights into the cultural and artistic significance of manga in Japan and around the world.

Interactive Manga Experience

The Kyoto International Manga Museum offers various interactive activities and events, such as drawing workshops, manga creation lessons, and cosplay events. Visitors can also try their hand at creating manga characters or participate in storytelling activities.

Research and Scholarship

The museum is not only a place for entertainment but also serves as a research facility. It hosts academic conferences and seminars related to manga and supports manga-related research projects.

Manga Cafés and Shops

The museum has manga cafés where visitors can relax and enjoy reading their favorite titles while sipping on refreshments. There are also manga-themed souvenir shops, offering a wide range of manga-related merchandise, books, and collectibles.

International Appeal

The museum attracts visitors from all over the world, making it a cultural hub for manga enthusiasts and a place to exchange ideas and experiences related to this unique art form.

Cultural Significance

Manga is an integral part of modern Japanese culture and has a significant impact on global popular culture. The Kyoto International Manga Museum celebrates this cultural phenomenon, recognizing its influence on storytelling, art, and entertainment.

The Museum of Kyoto

The Museum of Kyoto, also known as Kyoto City Museum, is a prominent cultural institution in Kyoto, Japan. It is dedicated to preserving and showcasing the history, art, and cultural heritage of Kyoto, a city with a rich and profound historical background. The museum offers a comprehensive view of Kyoto's past and present, making it a valuable destination for both locals and tourists seeking to deepen their understanding of the city's unique cultural identity.

History and Location

The Museum of Kyoto was established in 1928 and is located in the heart of the city, near the intersection of Sanjo-dori and Kawaramachi-dori. The museum's building itself holds historical significance, as it was originally constructed in the early 20th century as the Bank of Japan Kyoto Branch.

Permanent and Special Exhibitions

The museum's permanent exhibitions cover various aspects of Kyoto's history, culture, and traditions. It features a wide range of artifacts, artworks, historical documents, traditional crafts, and archaeological findings that span different periods of Kyoto's history. The exhibits are carefully curated to provide insights into the city's evolution, from its ancient origins to its modern transformation.

In addition to the permanent displays, the Museum of Kyoto hosts temporary special exhibitions that delve deeper into specific themes, artists, or historical eras. These special exhibitions offer fresh perspectives on Kyoto's cultural heritage and attract art enthusiasts and history lovers alike.

Kyoto's Cultural Heritage

The museum places a strong emphasis on Kyoto's cultural heritage, including its traditional crafts, performing arts, tea ceremonies, festivals, and architecture. Through exhibits and displays, visitors can gain a deeper appreciation for the cultural practices and artistic traditions that have shaped Kyoto's identity over the centuries.

Interactive and Educational Programs

The Museum of Kyoto offers various interactive and educational programs, workshops, and events for visitors of all ages. These activities aim to engage the public and promote a deeper understanding and appreciation of Kyoto's cultural heritage.

Community Engagement

The museum actively engages with the local community, collaborating with artists, researchers, and organizations to promote cultural exchange and preserve Kyoto's intangible cultural heritage.

Cultural Events and Performances

In addition to exhibitions and educational programs, the Museum of Kyoto hosts cultural events, traditional performances, and lectures that offer a taste of Kyoto's vibrant arts and cultural scene.

Cultural Significance

The Museum of Kyoto plays a crucial role in safeguarding and promoting Kyoto's cultural heritage, serving as a repository of its history and traditions. It allows locals and visitors to connect with the city's past and present, fostering a sense of pride and appreciation for Kyoto's unique cultural identity.

Kyoto Railway Museum

The Kyoto Railway Museum is a fascinating and engaging museum dedicated to the history and development of railways in Japan. Located in Shimogyo Ward, Kyoto, the museum is a paradise for railway enthusiasts and visitors interested in the country's transportation heritage. It offers a comprehensive and interactive experience that allows visitors to explore the evolution of Japan's railways and immerse themselves in the world of trains.

History and Location

The Kyoto Railway Museum was opened in 2016 by West Japan Railway Company (JR West). It is situated near Kyoto Station, making it easily accessible to tourists and locals alike.

Extensive Collection of Trains

The museum boasts an extensive collection of trains from various eras, showcasing the evolution of railway technology in Japan. Visitors can marvel at the beautifully preserved steam locomotives, vintage electric trains, and modern high-speed shinkansen (bullet trains). The exhibits cover a wide range of train types, from local commuter trains to luxurious sleeping cars used in long-distance travel.

Train Simulator Rides

One of the highlights of the Kyoto Railway Museum is the opportunity to experience train simulator rides. Visitors can step into the driver's seat of a realistic train simulator and get a taste of what it's like to operate a train on different routes and terrains.

Hands-On Exhibits

The museum offers a variety of interactive and hands-on exhibits that appeal to visitors of all ages. Visitors can try their hand at operating model trains, participate in railway-themed games and puzzles, and learn about the mechanics and engineering behind trains.

Historical Train Garage

The museum features a historical train garage where visitors can see the behind-the-scenes workings of maintaining and repairing trains. The garage also hosts special events and workshops related to railway maintenance and restoration.

Educational Programs

The Kyoto Railway Museum offers educational programs for school groups and families, providing informative and engaging activities that promote a deeper understanding of Japan's railway history and technology.

Outdoor Exhibits

In addition to the indoor exhibits, the museum has an outdoor display area where visitors can explore the exteriors of larger trains and even enter some of the preserved train carriages.

Cultural Significance

The Kyoto Railway Museum celebrates Japan's deep affinity with trains and its pioneering role in railway technology. Trains have played a crucial role in shaping Japan's modernization and transportation infrastructure, and the museum pays homage to this integral part of the country's history.

Nijo Castle Historical Museum

The Nijo Castle Historical Museum, also known as the Nijo Jinya Historical Museum, is a museum located within the

Nijo Castle complex in Kyoto, Japan. The museum showcases the history and cultural significance of Nijo Castle, a UNESCO World Heritage Site and one of Kyoto's most iconic landmarks. It offers visitors a glimpse into the castle's storied past, its architectural features, and the historical events that have taken place within its walls.

History and Location

Nijo Castle was built in 1603 as the residence of Tokugawa Ieyasu, the founder of the Tokugawa Shogunate, and completed in 1626. It was later used as an official residence for the Tokugawa Shoguns during their visits to Kyoto. The Nijo Castle Historical Museum was established to preserve and showcase the historical significance of this iconic structure.

Exhibits and Artifacts

The museum features a collection of artifacts, historical documents, and artworks that provide insights into the castle's history and the lives of the Tokugawa shoguns who resided there. Visitors can explore the architectural design and structural features of the castle, including its famous "nightingale floors" designed to alert occupants of potential intruders.

Historical Events

Nijo Castle has witnessed many significant historical events, and the museum offers information on the political and cultural context of the Edo period (1603-1868). It highlights the connections between the Tokugawa Shogunate and the imperial court, as well as the influence of the Tokugawa rule on the development of Kyoto and Japan as a whole.

Beautiful Gardens and Grounds

In addition to the museum, visitors can enjoy the stunning gardens and scenic grounds surrounding Nijo Castle. The gardens are designed in traditional Japanese style and offer a serene and tranquil environment.

Cultural and Architectural Significance

Nijo Castle is an excellent example of traditional Japanese castle architecture, and the museum highlights the castle's cultural and architectural significance. The castle's architecture represents the Momoyama and Edo periods' architectural styles and is a designated National Treasure of Japan.

Audio Guides and Interpretation

The Nijo Castle Historical Museum provides audio guides and interpretative materials in multiple languages to enhance the visitor experience and offer in-depth information about the castle's history and cultural importance.

Accessibility

The museum and Nijo Castle grounds are easily accessible by public transportation, making it a popular destination for tourists exploring Kyoto's historical sites.

Kyoto Museum of Modern Art

The Kyoto Museum of Modern Art, also known as Kyoto City KYOCERA Museum of Art, is a prominent cultural institution in Kyoto, Japan, dedicated to contemporary and modern art. The museum showcases a diverse collection of artworks, including paintings, sculptures, prints, and other forms of visual arts, created by both Japanese and international artists. It offers visitors a unique opportunity to explore the evolution of modern art and its impact on Japanese culture and society.

History and Location

The Kyoto Museum of Modern Art was founded in 1933 as the Kyoto Municipal Museum of Art. It underwent renovations and expansions over the years and reopened as the Kyoto City KYOCERA Museum of Art in 2020. The museum is situated in Okazaki Park, near Heian Shrine and other cultural landmarks, making it a convenient stop for visitors exploring Kyoto's cultural sites.

Collections and Exhibitions

The museum's collection comprises a wide range of modern and contemporary artworks, representing various artistic movements and styles. It includes works by influential

Japanese artists, as well as renowned international artists. Visitors can enjoy a diverse array of paintings, sculptures, ceramics, prints, and multimedia installations.

The museum hosts rotating exhibitions throughout the year, featuring both temporary exhibitions and highlights from its permanent collection. These exhibitions often explore different themes, artistic genres, and artists, offering fresh perspectives on modern art.

Japanese Modern Art

The Kyoto Museum of Modern Art plays a vital role in promoting and preserving Japanese modern art. It features works from the early 20th century onward, illustrating the development of modernism in Japan and the influence of Western artistic movements on Japanese artists.

Educational Programs and Activities

The museum offers educational programs, workshops, and lectures to engage visitors and provide a deeper understanding of the artworks and the artists' creative processes. These activities aim to foster an appreciation for modern art and encourage visitors to explore their own artistic expression.

Cultural Events

In addition to its exhibitions and educational programs, the museum hosts cultural events, art festivals, and special activities that enrich the visitor experience and promote cultural exchange.

Cultural Significance

The Kyoto Museum of Modern Art contributes to the cultural vibrancy of Kyoto by providing a platform for contemporary artists and celebrating the legacy of modern art. It reflects the city's commitment to preserving and promoting artistic and cultural diversity.

Kyoto Samurai and Ninja Museum

The Kyoto Samurai and Ninja Museum is an interactive and immersive museum located in Kyoto, Japan, that provides visitors with a hands-on experience into the world of samurai and ninja warriors. The museum offers a unique opportunity to learn about the history, skills, and traditions of these legendary figures from feudal Japan.

Interactive Exhibits

The Kyoto Samurai and Ninja Museum features interactive exhibits that allow visitors to dress up in traditional samurai armor or ninja attire. Visitors can experience the feeling of being a samurai or ninja warrior as they handle authentic weapons and try their hand at various martial arts techniques.

Ninja Experience

For those interested in the mysterious world of ninja warriors, the museum offers a ninja experience, where visitors can learn about stealth techniques, shuriken (throwing stars), and other tools used by ninja in their covert operations.

Samurai Swordsmanship

The museum provides opportunities to participate in samurai swordsmanship lessons, allowing visitors to practice the art of swordplay under the guidance of experienced instructors.

Historical Insights

The Kyoto Samurai and Ninja Museum also provides educational information about the history and lifestyle of samurai and ninja during Japan's feudal era. Visitors can learn about the code of conduct for samurai (bushido) and the various skills that ninja employed in their espionage and assassination missions.

Cultural Performances

In addition to interactive exhibits, the museum hosts cultural performances, such as traditional sword demonstrations, martial arts displays, and theatrical presentations, showcasing the skills and talents of samurai and ninja warriors.

Souvenir Shop

The museum includes a souvenir shop where visitors can purchase authentic samurai and ninja-related merchandise, including traditional weaponry, armor replicas, and other mementos.

Cultural Significance

The Kyoto Samurai and Ninja Museum plays a role in preserving and promoting Japan's historical and cultural heritage associated with samurai and ninja. It offers visitors from Japan and around the world an opportunity to connect with the fascinating history and traditions of these legendary figures.

KYOTO STATUES

Kyoto is home to various statues that hold cultural, historical, and artistic significance. While it's challenging to mention all of them, here are some notable statues you might want to see during your visit:

Miyako Odori Dancers

The Miyako Odori is an annual traditional dance performance held in Kyoto during the cherry blossom season (April) by geisha and maiko (apprentice geisha). It is one of the most famous and highly anticipated cultural events in Kyoto, attracting both locals and tourists from around the world.

During the Miyako Odori, geisha and maiko from the five geisha districts of Kyoto (known as hanamachi) come together to showcase their graceful dance performances. The event is held at the Gion Kobu Kaburenjo Theater, which is located in the Gion district, Kyoto's most well-known geisha district.

The performance typically consists of several acts that highlight traditional Japanese dance, music, and poetry. The dances are accompanied by live music played on traditional instruments, such as shamisen (a three-stringed instrument), taiko drums, and flutes.

The Miyako Odori performance often incorporates themes related to the beauty of the cherry blossoms and the changing seasons, reflecting the appreciation of nature in Japanese culture.

For those interested in experiencing Kyoto's geisha culture and traditional performing arts, attending the Miyako Odori is a wonderful opportunity. However, tickets for the performances can be in high demand, so it's advisable to book in advance, especially during the cherry blossom season when the city is bustling with visitors.

Senbon Shakado Kannon Statue

Located at the Senbon Shakado Temple, this large wooden Kannon statue is a National Treasure of Japan and is renowned for its exquisite craftsmanship.

Kukai (Kobo Daishi) Statue at To-ji

To-ji Temple houses a large bronze statue of Kukai, also known as Kobo Daishi, the founder of Shingon Buddhism. This impressive statue is an essential part of the temple's cultural significance.

Saigyo Modoshi no Matsu Statue

Located in Arashiyama, this statue commemorates the famous poet-monk Saigyo, who was known for his pilgrimage to various places, including Arashiyama.

Amida Buddha at Koryu-ji

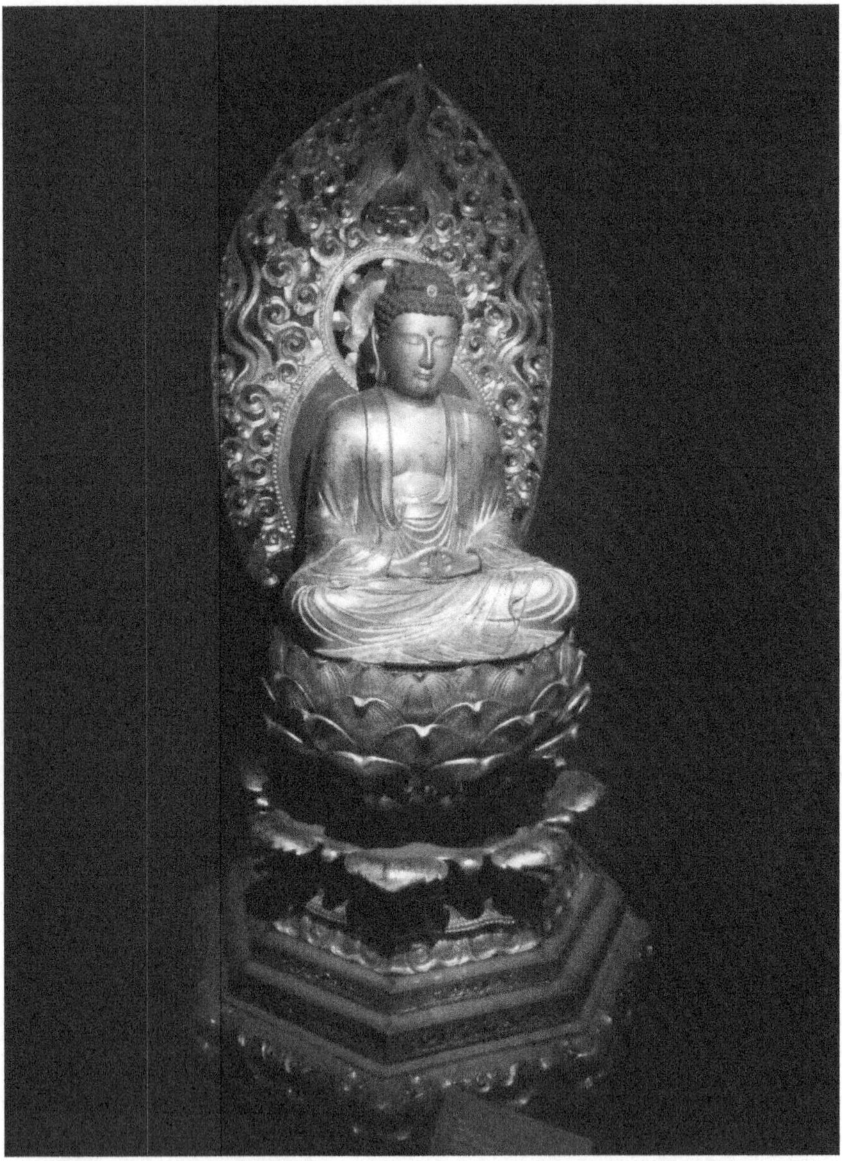

Koryu-ji, also known as Uzumasa Kannon, houses an Amida Buddha statue in Kyoto, Japan. This temple is located in the Ukyo ward of Kyoto and is considered one of the oldest temples in the city. The Amida Buddha statue at Koryu-ji is particularly noteworthy due to its historical significance and exquisite craftsmanship.

The Amida Buddha statue at Koryu-ji is a wooden statue, and it dates back to the early 7th century, making it a valuable and ancient artifact. This statue is designated as a National Treasure of Japan, showcasing its cultural importance and the level of reverence it holds in the country's history.

Koryu-ji Temple itself is renowned for being one of the oldest Zen temples in Kyoto and is a significant location for those interested in exploring the early history of Buddhism in Japan.

When visiting Koryu-ji and the Amida Buddha statue, take some time to appreciate the artistry and historical significance of this ancient representation of Amida Buddha. As with any cultural and historical site in Kyoto, remember to show respect and follow any guidelines provided by the temple authorities during your visit.

Statue of Tokugawa Ieyasu at Sanjusangendo

Sanjusangendo Temple features a statue of Tokugawa Ieyasu, the founder of the Tokugawa Shogunate, among its thousand standing Kannon statues.

Ryozen Kannon Statue

The Ryozen Kannon Statue, also known as the Ryozen Gokoku Shrine, is a significant landmark and memorial in Kyoto, Japan. It is a massive white concrete representation of the Bodhisattva Kannon, a compassionate figure in Buddhist belief, and it stands at an impressive height of approximately 24 meters (about 79 feet).

The statue was built to commemorate the Japanese soldiers who lost their lives during World War II. It was completed in 1955, with the intention of honoring and praying for the souls of the fallen soldiers. The Ryozen Kannon is also sometimes referred to as the "Kannon for Peace" due to its message of peace and hope for a harmonious future.

The statue is located on Ryozen Hill, providing a scenic view of Kyoto city. It's a solemn and peaceful place where visitors can pay their respects, offer prayers, and reflect on the sacrifices made during the war.

In addition to the Kannon statue, the Ryozen Gokoku Shrine complex also includes a war memorial and a museum dedicated to preserving the memory of those who perished in the war. The museum exhibits historical artifacts and documents related to the conflict.

For visitors interested in history, peace, and contemplation, the Ryozen Kannon Statue and Shrine offer a unique and poignant experience in Kyoto. As with any memorial site, it's essential to approach it with respect and reverence for the significance it holds in Japanese history and culture.

Maneki-neko (Beckoning Cat) Statue

The Maneki-neko, also known as the Beckoning Cat or Lucky Cat, is a popular and iconic Japanese figurine that is often displayed in shops, restaurants, and homes to bring good luck and prosperity. The Maneki-neko is typically depicted as a cat with one paw raised in a beckoning gesture.

The raised paw of the Maneki-neko is believed to invite good fortune and attract customers and wealth. The figurine is usually adorned with various decorations, such as a collar with bells, a bib, and a koban (an oval-shaped coin) held in the other paw, symbolizing wealth and prosperity.

The Maneki-neko comes in different colors, and each color represents a different kind of luck:

❖ Calico or tricolor (white, black, and orange): Brings overall good luck and prosperity.

❖ White: Represents purity and brings good fortune and happiness.

❖ Black: Guards against evil and illness.

❖ Gold: Attracts wealth and prosperity.

❖ Green: Ensures success in academics and studies.

❖ Red: Provides protection against evil spirits and illnesses.

In Kyoto, like in many other cities in Japan, you can find Maneki-neko statues and figurines in various places, especially in areas with a lot of shops and businesses. They are often displayed at the entrance or near the cashier, welcoming customers and bringing luck to the establishment.

Japanese Statue Moss

In Kyoto, Japan, you can find several famous moss-covered statues and monuments. The lush green moss adds a unique and serene charm to these ancient sculptures, enhancing their beauty and historical ambiance. Two well-known moss-covered statues in Kyoto are:

Moss-covered Kannon Statue at Kokedera (Moss Temple)

Kokedera, officially known as Saiho-ji Temple, is famous for its stunning moss garden and the moss-covered Kannon statue located within the temple complex. The temple's moss garden is considered one of the most beautiful and famous in Japan. Visitors can participate in a traditional ritual before gaining access to the garden to maintain its tranquility and protect the moss.

Moss-covered Jizo Statues at Otagi Nenbutsu-ji Temple

Otagi Nenbutsu-ji is a unique and less well-known temple in Kyoto, renowned for its collection of over 1,200 whimsical and moss-covered Jizo statues. Each statue is individually carved and showcases various facial expressions, making the temple grounds an enchanting and playful place to explore.

KYOTO'S MODERN SIDE

While Kyoto is renowned for its historical and traditional aspects, the city also has a vibrant and modern side that complements its ancient charm. Here are some aspects of Kyoto's modern side:

Modern Architecture

Kyoto is not only home to ancient temples and traditional wooden structures but also features modern architectural marvels. The Kyoto Station building, designed by architect Hiroshi Hara, is an impressive blend of futuristic design and functionality. Other modern architectural highlights include the Kyoto International Conference Center and the Kyoto Concert Hall.

Shopping and Entertainment

Kyoto offers a range of modern shopping and entertainment options. The Shijo-Kawaramachi area is a bustling commercial district with department stores, fashion boutiques, and trendy cafes. The Teramachi and Shinkyogoku shopping arcades are popular destinations for fashion, accessories, and local goods. Kyoto also has several modern multiplex cinemas, theaters, and concert halls that host a variety of performances.

Contemporary Art and Design

Kyoto has a thriving contemporary art and design scene. The Kyoto Art Center and Kyoto City University of Arts are important hubs for modern and experimental art exhibitions. The city also hosts the Kyoto International Film and Art Festival, which showcases contemporary films and artworks from around the world.

Cafe Culture

Kyoto boasts a vibrant cafe culture, with numerous modern and stylish cafes scattered throughout the city. From traditional tea houses serving matcha to chic coffee shops,

Kyoto offers a variety of options for coffee enthusiasts and those looking for a cozy place to relax.

Technology and Innovation

Kyoto is known as a center for technological advancements and innovation. The city is home to several research institutions, technology companies, and start-up incubators. Kyoto is also recognized for its expertise in green technology and sustainable initiatives, with projects focused on renewable energy, eco-friendly transportation, and environmental preservation.

Festivals and Events

Kyoto hosts various modern festivals and events that celebrate contemporary culture. The Kyoto International Manga Anime Fair is a major event dedicated to Japanese manga and anime, attracting fans from around the world. The Kyoto Experiment is a performing arts festival that showcases avant-garde and experimental theater, dance, and music performances.

Gastronomy

While Kyoto is known for its traditional cuisine, the city also embraces modern gastronomic trends. You can find a range of international restaurants, fusion cuisine, and innovative dining experiences that blend traditional Japanese flavors with contemporary techniques.

SHOPPING IN KYOTO

Kyoto's Shopping Streets

Kyoto is home to several vibrant shopping streets and arcades where you can find a wide range of goods, from traditional crafts to modern fashion. These shopping streets offer a mix of local charm and contemporary appeal, making them popular destinations for both locals and tourists. Here are some of Kyoto's notable shopping streets:

Teramachi-dori

Located in the heart of Kyoto's city center, Teramachi-dori is a covered shopping arcade filled with shops selling clothing, accessories, crafts, electronics, and more. You can find both traditional and modern goods here, making it a great place for shopping and exploring.

Shinkyogoku-dori

Adjacent to Teramachi-dori, Shinkyogoku-dori is another covered shopping arcade that runs parallel to it. This bustling street offers a mix of fashion boutiques, souvenir shops, and restaurants, making it a popular spot for both shopping and dining.

Nishiki Market

Known as "Kyoto's Kitchen," Nishiki Market is a historic and lively food market that stretches for several blocks. Here, you can find an array of fresh seafood, vegetables, fruits, snacks, sweets, and traditional Kyoto cuisine ingredients.

Kawaramachi-dori

Kawaramachi-dori is a major shopping street running along the Kamo River. It's a bustling area with numerous department stores, fashion boutiques, and shops selling a variety of goods. This street is popular among young people for shopping and entertainment.

Sanjo-dori

Sanjo-dori is a vibrant street lined with shops, cafes, and restaurants. It's known for its fashionable boutiques and trendy stores, making it a popular spot for fashion enthusiasts.

Kitano Tenmangu Shrine Flea Market

On the 25th of each month, the area around Kitano Tenmangu Shrine hosts a flea market where vendors sell antiques, crafts, second-hand goods, and more. It's a unique opportunity to find some hidden treasures.

Takoyakushi-dori

This shopping street connects Shijo-dori to Gion and is known for its traditional atmosphere. You can find kimono shops, craft stores, tea houses, and souvenir shops along this quaint street.

Kiyamachi-dori

Running parallel to the Kamo River, Kiyamachi-dori is a charming street lined with traditional machiya houses converted into bars, restaurants, and shops. It's a popular area for nightlife and dining.

Kiyomizu-zaka and Sannen-zaka

These streets lead up to the famous Kiyomizu-dera Temple and are lined with shops selling traditional crafts, souvenirs, and local snacks. The traditional buildings and narrow lanes add to the charm of these streets.

Kyoto Station Building

The Kyoto Station building itself is a shopping destination, housing various shops and boutiques, including souvenir shops offering Kyoto-themed gifts and crafts.

Shopping at Nishiki Market

Nishiki Market, often referred to as "Kyoto's Kitchen," is a bustling and historic food market located in the heart of Kyoto, Japan. It stretches for several blocks along Nishikikoji-dori, a narrow shopping street, and is one of the city's most famous and beloved markets. Nishiki Market has been a vital part of Kyoto's culinary culture for centuries, and it offers visitors a delightful experience of local flavors, traditional ingredients, and a vibrant atmosphere. Here are some key features of Nishiki Market:

Food Stalls and Shops

Nishiki Market is home to over a hundred food stalls, shops, and restaurants, each offering a wide variety of local and seasonal products. You can find fresh seafood, vegetables, fruits, pickles, sweets, Kyoto-style snacks, and other traditional Japanese ingredients.

Traditional Kyoto Cuisine

The market is an excellent place to sample traditional Kyoto cuisine, including dishes like yuba (tofu skin), tsukemono (pickles), matcha-flavored treats, fresh sashimi, grilled skewers, and more. Many shops offer free samples, allowing visitors to taste before they buy.

Seasonal Offerings

Nishiki Market's offerings change with the seasons, and you can find various seasonal delicacies depending on the time of your visit. This makes the market a dynamic and ever-changing destination.

Local Vendors

The market is known for its friendly and knowledgeable local vendors who take pride in their products and often share insights about Kyoto's culinary traditions.

Traditional Architecture

The market's covered shopping street features a mix of traditional machiya-style buildings and modern structures, creating a unique atmosphere that blends history with contemporary shopping.

Cultural Experience

Visiting Nishiki Market provides an authentic cultural experience as you immerse yourself in the bustling local scene and sample traditional Japanese foods.

Souvenirs and Gifts

Nishiki Market is an excellent place to shop for souvenirs and food-related gifts. You can find packaged local snacks, Kyoto-style sweets, traditional tea sets, and other unique items to take home with you.

Location

Nishiki Market is conveniently located in the central part of Kyoto, within walking distance from popular tourist spots such as Gion, Shijo-dori, and Kawaramachi-dori.

Kawaramachi-dori

Kawaramachi-dori is one of Kyoto's major shopping streets, located in the central part of the city. It runs parallel to the Kamo River and is a lively and bustling area known for its wide array of shops, restaurants, entertainment venues, and fashion boutiques. Kawaramachi-dori is a popular destination for both locals and tourists, offering a vibrant atmosphere and a diverse range of shopping and dining options. Here are some key features of Kawaramachi-dori:

Shopping

Kawaramachi-dori is a shopper's paradise, with numerous department stores, specialty shops, and fashion boutiques lining the street. Visitors can find a wide variety of goods, including clothing, accessories, cosmetics, electronics, traditional crafts, and more.

Fashion Boutiques

The street is particularly known for its fashion boutiques, offering the latest trends and styles. It's a popular spot for young people and fashion enthusiasts to explore the latest Japanese fashion.

Department Stores

Kawaramachi-dori is home to several department stores, including Takashimaya, Marui, and OPA, where you can find a curated selection of high-quality goods, luxury brands, and popular Japanese fashion.

Cafes and Restaurants: There are numerous cafes, restaurants, and food establishments along Kawaramachi-dori, offering a wide range of cuisines, from traditional Japanese dishes to international flavors.

Entertainment: In addition to shopping and dining, Kawaramachi-dori offers various entertainment options, including movie theaters, karaoke establishments, and game centers.

Street Performances: During certain times of the year, you may encounter street performances and events along Kawaramachi-dori, adding to the lively and festive atmosphere of the street.

Convenient Location: Kawaramachi-dori is conveniently located in the central part of Kyoto, making it easily accessible from various parts of the city and a popular spot for both locals and tourists to gather and enjoy.

Kamo River: The street runs parallel to the scenic Kamo River, providing opportunities for a leisurely stroll along the riverbanks and enjoying the natural beauty of Kyoto.

Handmade Crafts

Handmade crafts are a treasured aspect of Kyoto's cultural heritage, known for their exquisite craftsmanship, attention to detail, and traditional techniques passed down through generations. The city's artisans create a wide range of handmade crafts, each with its unique beauty and significance. Here are some of the most notable handmade crafts you can find in Kyoto:

Kyoto Pottery (Kyo-yaki/Kiyomizu-yaki)

Kyoto is famous for its pottery, known as Kyo-yaki or Kiyomizu-yaki. Skilled potters create beautiful ceramics, including tea sets, vases, plates, and decorative objects. The unique glazing and elegant designs make these pieces highly prized by collectors and tea ceremony enthusiasts.

Yuzen and Kyo-Yuzen Textiles

Kyo-yuzen is a traditional dyeing technique used to create intricate and vibrant designs on kimono fabrics. Artisans skillfully hand-paint and dye patterns inspired by nature and Japanese motifs. Yuzen textiles are often used for kimono, obi (sashes), and various textile products.

Washi Paper Crafts

Washi, traditional Japanese paper made from mulberry fibers, is used to create various crafts in Kyoto. You can find handmade washi products such as lanterns, stationery, decorative items, and art prints in specialty shops.

Kyoto Fans (Sensu and Uchiwa)

Kyoto is known for producing both sensu (folding fans) and uchiwa (round fans). Artisans carefully craft these fans, painting them with intricate designs and motifs. They make for beautiful souvenirs and gifts.

Japanese Calligraphy (Shodo)

Kyoto has a strong tradition of calligraphy, with skilled calligraphers creating stunning works of art using brush and ink. Calligraphy scrolls and framed pieces are available for purchase.

Bamboo Crafts

Kyoto artisans use bamboo to create a wide range of products, including baskets, tea utensils, and decorative items. Bamboo craftwork showcases the natural beauty of this versatile material.

Traditional Dolls (Hina-ningyo and Kokeshi)

Kyoto is known for its exquisite Hina-ningyo (Girls' Day dolls) and Kokeshi dolls. These handmade dolls represent traditional Japanese culture and are displayed during specific festivals and celebrations.

Kumihimo (Japanese Braids)

Kumihimo is a traditional braiding technique used to create beautiful cords and accessories. You can find kumihimo products like bracelets, necklaces, and keychains.

Metalwork

Kyoto's metalworkers create fine metal crafts, such as tea ceremony utensils, decorative items, and traditional metal ornaments.

Lacquerware: Artisans in Kyoto produce exquisite lacquerware, applying layers of natural lacquer to wooden bases to create durable and beautiful items like bowls, trays, and boxes.

Antique Shops

Kyoto is a city rich in history and cultural heritage, making it a fantastic destination for antique enthusiasts. There are several antique shops and markets scattered throughout the city where you can discover a diverse array of authentic and unique antiques. Whether you are looking for traditional Japanese artifacts, vintage items, or unique souvenirs, Kyoto's antique shops offer a treasure trove of finds. Here are some places to explore:

Kamigamo Shrine Antique Fair

Held on the 25th of each month at Kamigamo Shrine, this monthly antique fair features a variety of vendors selling antiques, vintage items, and traditional crafts.

Tomioka Hachimangu Shrine Antique Fair

Another monthly antique fair held on the 15th of each month at Tomioka Hachimangu Shrine, offering a selection of antiques and second-hand goods.

Kitano Tenmangu Shrine Flea Market

On the 25th of each month, this flea market is held at Kitano Tenmangu Shrine, showcasing a diverse range of antiques and collectibles.

Kougei Koubou Ishibutai

This antique shop specializes in traditional Japanese crafts and artifacts, offering a selection of ceramics, textiles, and lacquerware.

Gion Nishikawa

Located in Gion, this shop specializes in antique kimono and obi, perfect for those looking to bring home a piece of Japanese heritage.

Yasaka-jinja Shrine Flea Market

On the 18th and 25th of each month, this flea market at Yasaka-jinja Shrine offers a mix of antiques, crafts, and vintage items.

Mitsuisakauchi Antique Shop Street

This street in Kyoto is lined with various antique shops, where you can find a diverse collection of antiques, from ceramics to traditional art pieces.

Kougei no Honya Chion-in

This shop near Chion-in Temple specializes in traditional crafts and antiques, offering a wide range of items, including ceramics and woodwork.

Fuyacho Antique Mall

Situated in a historic machiya building, this antique mall houses multiple shops selling antiques and vintage goods.

Kyoto Antiques Center

Located in a modern building, this center houses a variety of shops selling antiques and traditional crafts.

Department Stores

Kyoto boasts several department stores, offering a diverse selection of goods, luxury brands, and popular Japanese products. These department stores are not only great places for shopping but also provide various dining and entertainment options. Here are some notable department stores in Kyoto:

Takashimaya Kyoto Store

Takashimaya is one of Japan's most renowned department store chains, and its Kyoto location is no exception. Situated in the heart of the city, near Kawaramachi-dori, Takashimaya Kyoto offers a wide range of luxury and designer brands, cosmetics, homeware, and traditional Japanese crafts. The basement floor is dedicated to a gourmet food hall, where you can find a delightful array of local and international cuisine.

Daimaru Kyoto

Another prominent department store, Daimaru Kyoto, is located near Kyoto Station. It features multiple floors of fashion, accessories, beauty products, and lifestyle goods. Daimaru also hosts seasonal events and promotions, making it a vibrant shopping destination.

Mitsukoshi Kyoto

Mitsukoshi is another well-known department store chain, and its Kyoto location is found in the Shijo-Kawaramachi area. The store offers an array of luxury brands, traditional crafts, and food products, along with dining options and event spaces.

Isetan Kyoto

Isetan is a Japanese department store known for its high-quality merchandise and fashion selections. The Isetan Kyoto store is situated in the Kyoto Station building, making it a convenient stop for travelers. It offers fashion, cosmetics, and lifestyle products, as well as a food hall with a variety of gourmet items.

JR Kyoto Isetan

Located within the Kyoto Station building, JR Kyoto Isetan is another section of the Isetan department store. It focuses primarily on fashion, accessories, and beauty products.

Yodobashi Kyoto

Yodobashi is a large electronics and home appliances store, where you can find the latest gadgets, cameras, computers, and more. The Kyoto store is near Kyoto Station and is an ideal spot for tech enthusiasts.

Flea Markets and Craft Fairs

Kyoto is a city that loves its traditional arts and crafts, and flea markets and craft fairs are excellent opportunities to discover unique and authentic handmade products. These events often take place at temples, shrines, and public spaces, providing a chance to not only shop for local crafts but also experience the cultural ambiance of Kyoto. Here are some flea markets and craft fairs you can explore in Kyoto:

To-ji Temple Flea Market

Held on the 21st of each month, the To-ji Temple Flea Market is one of the largest and most famous flea markets in Kyoto. It features a wide range of antiques, handicrafts, clothing, and second-hand goods.

Kobo-san Market at To-ji Temple

Taking place on the 21st of each month along with the flea market, the Kobo-san Market is dedicated to arts and crafts, offering a variety of handmade products made by local artisans.

Tenjin-san Market at Kitano Tenmangu Shrine

Held on the 25th of each month, this market offers a mix of antiques, crafts, and second-hand items. It's a fantastic opportunity to explore the historic Kitano Tenmangu Shrine and shop for unique goods.

Kamigamo Shrine Antique Fair

Taking place on the 25th of each month, this fair features vendors selling antiques, traditional crafts, and vintage items.

Tomioka Hachimangu Shrine Antique Fair

Held on the 15th of each month, this antique fair offers a variety of antiques and second-hand goods.

Handmade in Kyoto Craft Fair

This craft fair is held at Kyoto International Community House and showcases handmade crafts made by local artisans. It's a great place to find unique gifts and souvenirs.

Kyoto Artisan Market at Heian Shrine

Held on selected weekends throughout the year, this market gathers artisans from all over Japan, showcasing their handmade crafts, pottery, textiles, and more.

Kyoto Handicraft Center

Although not a flea market or craft fair, the Kyoto Handicraft Center is a permanent venue where you can find an extensive selection of traditional crafts and handmade products from Kyoto and beyond.

Traditional Tea Shops

Kyoto is renowned for its tea culture, and there are numerous traditional tea shops throughout the city where you can experience the art of tea and purchase high-quality Japanese teas and tea-related products. These tea shops offer a wide range of teas, including green tea, matcha, sencha, genmaicha, hojicha, and more. Here are some traditional tea shops in Kyoto to explore:

Ippodo Tea Co. (Main Store)

Ippodo is one of Kyoto's oldest and most prestigious tea shops, founded in 1717. They offer a wide variety of high-quality Japanese teas, including matcha, sencha, and gyokuro. You can also enjoy a traditional tea ceremony experience at their main store.

Fukujuen Kyoto Honten

Fukujuen is another well-established tea shop with a history dating back to 1790. They specialize in various tea varieties and offer tea tastings at their main store in the Gion district.

Marukyu Koyamaen

This tea shop in Uji, just outside of Kyoto, is famous for its matcha and has been in operation since 1688. They provide high-quality matcha products and offer tea ceremony experiences.

Uji-en Kyoto Store

Uji-en is known for its premium Uji tea, particularly matcha and gyokuro. The Kyoto store offers an array of tea products and tea sets.

Jugetsudo

Jugetsudo is a modern tea shop that specializes in organic and high-quality Japanese teas. They offer a variety of loose-leaf teas and tea-related products.

Kyoto Obubu Tea Farms

Located in the picturesque Wazuka tea-growing region near Kyoto, Obubu Tea Farms is a great place to learn about tea cultivation and purchase fresh, locally grown teas.

Kagizen Yoshifusa

Although primarily a traditional Japanese confectionery shop, Kagizen Yoshifusa also serves high-quality matcha in a serene tearoom setting.

Gion Tsujiri

Tsujiri is famous for its matcha-flavored sweets and beverages. At their Gion store, you can enjoy various matcha treats and purchase matcha products.

Itohkyuemon Kyoto Honten

This tea shop, established in 1832, offers a variety of Japanese teas, including matcha, sencha, and hojicha. They also have a café where you can enjoy tea and sweets.

Kyoto Station Building

The Kyoto Station Building is a modern and iconic landmark in Kyoto, serving as a major transportation hub and a commercial complex. It is one of Japan's largest railway stations and is known for its striking architectural design. The station is not just a transportation facility but also a popular destination in its own right, offering an array of shops, restaurants, and entertainment options. Here are some features and highlights of the Kyoto Station Building:

Architectural Design

Designed by architect Hiroshi Hara, the Kyoto Station Building's unique architectural style combines modernity with traditional Japanese elements. The station's roof is constructed in the shape of a wave, symbolizing harmony between the city's past and future.

Hachijo Gate

The main entrance of the station is the Hachijo Gate, where you can witness the impressive architecture and the iconic "Big Tetsudo" clock hanging from the roof.

Transportation Hub

Kyoto Station serves as a central transportation hub, connecting various train lines, including the Shinkansen (bullet train) lines, JR lines, and private railway lines. It is the gateway for travelers arriving in Kyoto from major cities like Tokyo and Osaka.

Isetan Department Store

Within the station building, you'll find the Kyoto branch of the Isetan department store. This popular department store offers a wide range of fashion, cosmetics, homeware, and food products.

Porta Underground Shopping Mall

The Porta shopping mall is located underground and houses various shops, boutiques, and eateries. It's a convenient place to shop and dine while waiting for trains.

Skyway and Star Road

The Skyway is a pedestrian walkway on the 11th floor, offering panoramic views of the station and the surrounding city. The Star Road escalator on the south side of the station is an illuminated staircase, creating a magical ambiance during the evening.

Kyoto Tower

Adjacent to Kyoto Station is the Kyoto Tower, another iconic landmark offering stunning views of the city from its observation deck.

Kyoto Station Building Rooftop Garden

The station building features a rooftop garden called "The Sky Garden," offering a green space for relaxation and enjoying views of the cityscape.

Cultural Events

The station occasionally hosts cultural events and exhibitions, providing visitors with an opportunity to experience traditional Japanese arts and crafts.

Gion

Gion is one of Kyoto's most famous and iconic districts, renowned for its traditional charm, historic streets, and association with geisha and maiko culture. It is a must-visit destination for anyone exploring Kyoto, as it provides a glimpse into the city's rich cultural heritage. Here are some key features and highlights of Gion:

Geisha and Maiko Culture

Gion is known for its association with the geisha and maiko (apprentice geisha) culture. Geisha are skilled entertainers who perform traditional Japanese arts such as music, dance, and conversation. You may catch a glimpse of geisha and maiko dressed in their elaborate kimono and hairstyles, particularly in the evenings when they are on their way to tea houses and entertainment venues.

Historic Streets

The streets of Gion are lined with beautifully preserved traditional wooden machiya buildings and narrow alleyways, creating a nostalgic atmosphere reminiscent of old Kyoto. Hanami-koji and Shirakawa-minami-dori are two of the most picturesque streets in Gion.

Teahouses and Restaurants

Gion is home to numerous teahouses and exclusive restaurants where you can experience traditional Japanese hospitality and cuisine. Some teahouses offer authentic tea ceremonies, while others provide exquisite kaiseki (traditional multi-course meals).

Yasaka Shrine

Located at the eastern end of Gion, Yasaka Shrine is an important Shinto shrine with a history dating back over a thousand years. The shrine is especially lively during festivals and events.

Gion Corner

For a condensed experience of traditional arts, consider visiting Gion Corner, where performances of tea ceremonies, flower arranging, koto music, and traditional dance are held regularly.

Kawakami Theater (Gion Kobu Kaburenjo)

This traditional theater hosts public performances of traditional Kyoto dance known as "Kyo-mai" by maiko and geisha.

Gion Matsuri Festival

Gion Matsuri is one of Japan's most famous festivals, held in July, and it showcases stunning floats and cultural events throughout the district.

Shops and Souvenirs

Gion is dotted with souvenir shops, art galleries, and boutiques selling traditional crafts, including ceramics, textiles, and local specialties.

Cherry Blossom Viewing

In spring, Gion becomes an enchanting spot for cherry blossom viewing, attracting locals and tourists alike to enjoy the blooming sakura trees along the Shirakawa Canal.

Geisha Experience

Some teahouses in Gion offer geisha experience programs for visitors, allowing you to dress up in kimono, have your makeup done, and enjoy tea and conversation with maiko.

Pontocho

Pontocho is a historic and atmospheric alleyway located in the heart of Kyoto, running parallel to the Kamo River. It is one of the most charming and picturesque areas in the city, known for its traditional architecture, narrow lanes, and vibrant nightlife. Pontocho is a popular destination for locals and tourists alike, offering a unique blend of old-world charm and modern entertainment. Here are some key features and highlights of Pontocho:

Traditional Architecture

Pontocho is lined with traditional wooden machiya buildings, some of which have been converted into restaurants, teahouses, bars, and entertainment venues. The lantern-lit alleyway exudes a nostalgic ambiance, particularly during the evenings.

Izakayas and Restaurants

Pontocho is famous for its many izakayas (Japanese-style pubs) and restaurants, offering a wide range of dining options, from traditional Japanese dishes to modern fusion cuisine. Many establishments have riverside terraces with scenic views of the Kamo River.

Geisha and Maiko Sightings

In the evenings, you may be lucky enough to spot geisha and maiko walking to their appointments along Pontocho's cobbled streets. However, please be respectful and avoid intruding on their privacy.

Kawayuka Dining

During the warmer months, many restaurants in Pontocho set up kawayuka, platforms over the Kamo River, where patrons can dine and enjoy the pleasant river breeze.

Nightlife

Pontocho comes alive at night, with lanterns illuminating the alleyway and creating a magical atmosphere. It's a great place to experience Kyoto's nightlife, whether you're looking for a relaxed drink at a cozy bar or want to enjoy live music performances.

Entertainment: Pontocho offers various forms of entertainment, including traditional performances, live music, and occasional street performances.

Cherry Blossom Viewing

During the cherry blossom season, Pontocho is a popular spot for hanami (cherry blossom viewing), as the cherry trees along the Kamo River create a stunning backdrop.

Cultural Heritage

Pontocho has been a significant part of Kyoto's cultural heritage for centuries and remains a symbol of the city's historic charm.

Souvenirs and Gifts

The shops in Pontocho offer a selection of Kyoto-themed souvenirs, traditional crafts, and unique gifts to take home.

River Cruises

From Pontocho, you can also embark on scenic river cruises along the Kamo River, providing a different perspective of Kyoto.

WHAT TO EAT

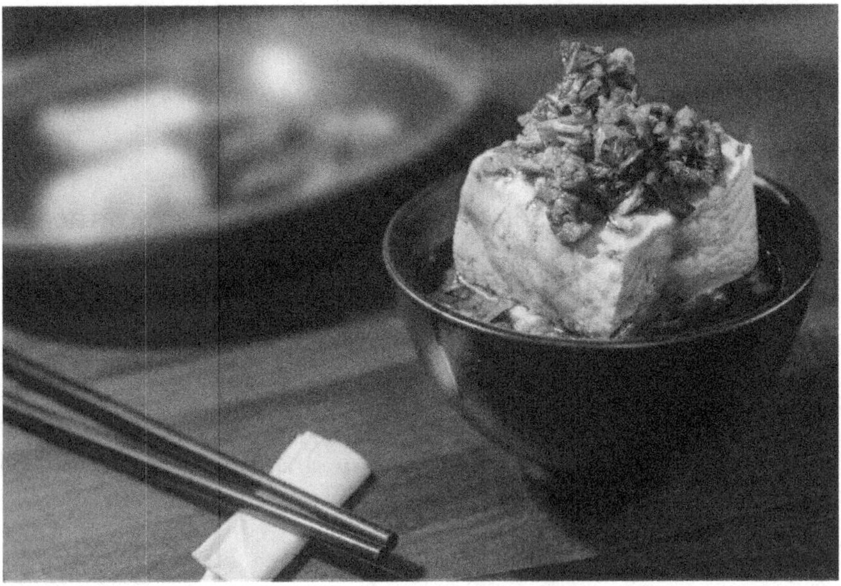

Kyoto, with its long-standing cultural heritage, is also renowned for its distinctive cuisine. Kyoto cuisine, known as "Kyo-ryori," emphasizes seasonal ingredients, refined flavors, and artful presentation. Here are some key elements and dishes of Kyoto cuisine:

Kaiseki Ryori

Kaiseki is a traditional multi-course meal that showcases the harmony of flavors, textures, and colors. It often consists of meticulously prepared small dishes, including appetizers, sashimi, simmered dishes, grilled items, and a seasonal soup. Kaiseki meals in Kyoto are particularly famous for their attention to detail and use of local ingredients.

Obanzai

Obanzai refers to the traditional home-cooked dishes of Kyoto. It consists of simple, flavorful, and seasonal dishes made with locally sourced ingredients. Obanzai dishes often include vegetables, tofu, and fish prepared in various ways, such as simmering, grilling, or frying.

Yudofu

Yudofu is a specialty of Kyoto and is especially popular during the winter months. It is a simple and elegant dish of tofu simmered in a light kombu (kelp) broth. The tofu is usually served with dipping sauces, such as ponzu (citrus-based sauce) or sesame sauce, and accompanied by a variety of seasonal vegetables.

Yuba

Yuba is a specialty of Kyoto and refers to the delicate skin that forms on the surface of heated soy milk. It is a prized ingredient and often used in various dishes such as yuba rolls, yuba sashimi, and yuba hot pots. Yuba is prized for its smooth texture and subtle flavor.

Matcha

Kyoto is famous for its high-quality matcha (powdered green tea). You can enjoy matcha in various forms, such as in tea ceremonies, traditional sweets (wagashi), matcha-flavored ice cream, and even savory dishes like matcha soba noodles.

Sushi

Kyoto is known for its unique style of sushi called "Otsukuri" or "Kyoto-style sushi." It typically features fresh, seasonal fish and seafood delicately arranged on bite-sized vinegar-seasoned rice. The emphasis is on simplicity and highlighting the natural flavors of the ingredients.

Kyoto Sweets

Kyoto has a long-standing tradition of crafting exquisite and artistic traditional sweets, known as "wagashi." These sweets often feature seasonal ingredients, such as sweet bean paste, matcha, and seasonal fruits. They are not only delicious but also visually appealing, reflecting Kyoto's emphasis on aesthetics.

WHERE TO EAT IN KYOTO

Tofu, matcha, bracken starch, and kudzu are just a few of the traditional Japanese ingredients found in Kyoto cuisine. For a city without land, it also has a lot of preserved seafood, like salt-pickled mackerel and dried herring.

There is tuna sushi and pickled sushi, both of which are delicious despite their odd appearances. Kaiseki is another traditional way to eat, with seasonal ingredients and a distinctly Japanese flavor. The dish also includes dashi and kombu. Japanese sweets like bracken flour mochi, matcha parfaits, and kudzu noodles are also delicious. When you visit the city, you should also think about trying some of the city's other famous restaurants, such as Udon. The Best Places to Eat in Tokyo:

Rai Rai Tei

Try the "standard ramen" and miso ramen that Rai Rai Tei has to offer. In Kyoto, Rai Rai Tei operates multiple restaurants.

Menya Inoichi Hanare

This is a Michelin Face cloth Gourmand ramen eatery that has some expertise in miso ramen made with one or the other white or dark soy sauce.

Wajouryoumen Sugari

Wajouryoumen Sugari Tsukemen is a type of ramen in which the noodles and broth are served separately. Before eating, dip the noodles in the broth, which is significantly more flavorful than regular ramen broth. This is done to make sure that the noodles get as much flavor as possible.

Kura Sushi

Kura Sushi is a well-known Japanese chain of Kaitenzushi restaurants. Kaitenzushi is a Japanese restaurant that serves sushi on conveyor belts. Customers are free to eat whatever they want at the restaurant, where sushi plates are provided at each table. In Japan, it is not only one of the cheapest but also one of the most entertaining ways to enjoy sushi.

Musashi Sushi

Sushi is a Kyoto-exclusive Kaitenzushi restaurant. Although it costs more than Kura, it is just as good.

Gion Kappa

Kappa is a lively and welcoming izakaya with small plates for JPY 390. In a lot of Japanese restaurants and Izakayas, customers must have an obligatory appetizer known as Otoshi. It is only available in establishments that offer alcohol and costs money. It could be thought of as a cover charge for things like food and drink.

Wadachi

Wadachi is a sake bar and restaurant within walking distance of Gion Kappa that welcomes gaijin patrons. It carries a wide selection of sakes from all over the nation. Each serving of sake costs JPY 500 (plus tax) at Wadachi.

Ibushigin Kazuya

Ibushigin Kazuya is within walking distance of the Kamo River and can be reached from either Gion-Shijo or Sanjo Station in about 6-7 minutes. One of the country's most mind-blowing purpose-creating regions is the Fushimi region in Kyoto.

Unagi Hirokawa

Hirokawa is a popular destination for unagi. Unagi refers to the barbecued freshwater eel. Before being slowly barbecued over charcoal and seasoned with kabayaki sauce (sweet soy sauce), the eel is pierced and cooked.

Hachidaime Gihey

This is a well-known Kyoto restaurant that offers reasonably priced set meals for lunch and kaiseki meals for dinner.

Donguri's Okonomiyaki

Donguri's Okonomiyaki is typically made with pork belly, seafood, vegetables, noodles, and green onions on a teppanyaki grill. Donguri, a local chain of okonomiyaki restaurants, is said by some to be the best in Kyoto.

Komefuku Shijo Karasuma

This is a fascinating tempura restaurant in Kyoto where you can order individual portions. Komefuku Shijo Karasuma is close to Karasuma Station. If you want tempura while you're in Kyoto, this is a great place to eat. Although Komefuku Shijo Karasuma's tempura sets are reasonably priced, tempura can be quite costly in Japan.

Nishiki Market

When in Kyoto, you must visit the Nishiki Market. As the name implies, the market's five-block covered area is surrounded by more than a hundred stores, Japanese street food vendors, and tavern-style eateries offering a variety of regional food items.

WHERE TO STAY IN KYOTO

You can stay in anything in Kyoto, from very affordable guesthouses to five-star hotels around the globe. Kyoto is a fantastic location to take advantage of this amazing "only in Japan" experience due to the plethora of ryokans, and traditional Japanese inns. Be mindful that staying in a nice ryokan can be very expensive (remember that they usually provide meals) and that it takes more work than staying in a hotel. I often advise tourists to Kyoto to stay in a ryokan on their first night before moving to a hotel for the rest of their stay. The best and most practical spots to remain in Kyoto are listed below in rough order, with the most practical areas listed first.

Downtown Kyoto

The finest area of the city to set up shop is generally Downtown Kyoto. The city's two railway lines, both subway lines, and hundreds of eateries, stores, and bars are all accessible on foot. Additionally, both the northern and southern Higashiyamas, two of Kyoto's main tourist destinations, are easily accessible from downtown.

Southern Higashiyama

Another great spot is southern Higashiyama. You'll be close to many of the city's most remarkable sites and a ton of eateries if you stay in or close to Gion. The greatest thing about Southern Higashiyama is that its streets are so evocative that you can stroll through them at night.

Northern Higashiyama

If you want to be close to greenery and don't mind riding a bus or bicycle to get downtown to dine and shop, Northern Higashiyama is an excellent location to stay (there are, of course, some restaurants in Northern Higashiyama). There are a few ryokan, guesthouses, and holiday rentals in Northern Higashiyama, but not many motels.

My Recommendation

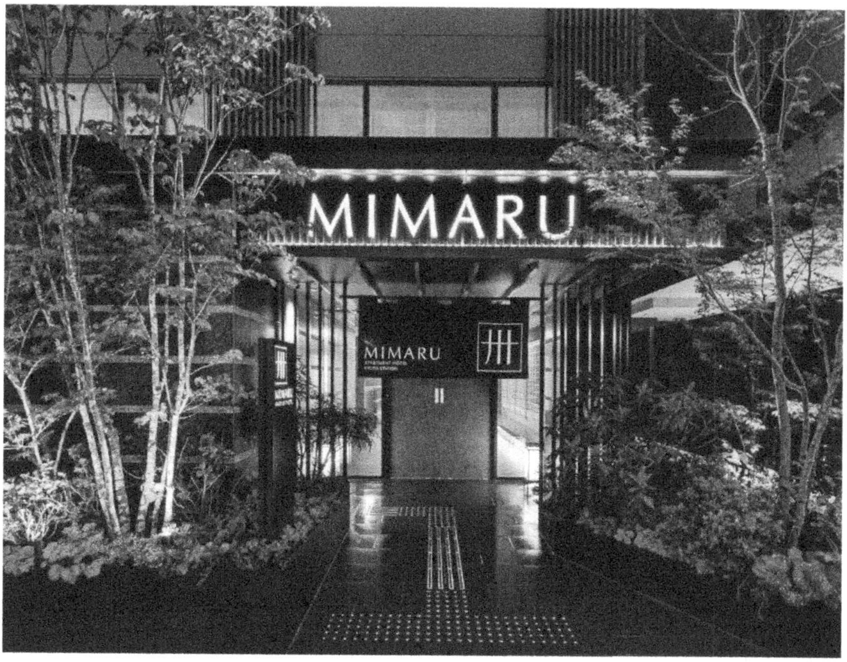

I recommend that you stay at MIMARU when visiting Kyoto. My experience at this serviced apartment was truly exceptional, and I believe it offers a unique and enriching way to experience the city.

First and foremost, the location of MIMARU in Kyoto was superb. It was situated in a quiet and charming neighborhood, yet still close enough to major attractions and public transportation. This allowed me to explore Kyoto's iconic sites conveniently while also getting a glimpse of the local life and culture.

The check-in process was smooth, and the staff was incredibly friendly and accommodating. They spoke English fluently, which was a huge plus for international travelers like me, as it made communication much easier.

The apartment itself was a pleasant surprise. It felt like a real home away from home, with a thoughtful combination of modern amenities and traditional Japanese elements. The interior was spacious, clean, and tastefully decorated, creating a cozy and welcoming ambiance. Having a kitchenette was a fantastic feature as well, as it allowed me to prepare simple meals and snacks during my stay.

One of the highlights of staying at MIMARU was the opportunity to experience a more authentic and immersive side of Kyoto. Unlike hotels, where you might feel somewhat detached from the local lifestyle, MIMARU made me feel like I was part of the community. I enjoyed going out in the morning to nearby local cafes and shops, interacting with residents, and feeling like I was truly living in Kyoto for a brief moment.

Additionally, the on-site amenities at MIMARU were top-notch. There was a communal area where I could relax and meet other guests, as well as a cozy library with a collection of books about Kyoto's history and culture. These little touches added an extra layer of charm to the overall experience.

Lastly, I must mention the value for money. Considering the level of comfort, the excellent service, and the prime location, the rates at MIMARU were quite reasonable, making it an excellent choice for budget-conscious travelers without compromising on quality.

KYOTO SHINKANSENS

Kyoto is well-connected to major cities in Japan through the Shinkansen, also known as the bullet train. The Shinkansen is a high-speed rail network that allows passengers to travel quickly and comfortably between cities. Here are some of the key Shinkansen lines that connect to Kyoto:

Tokaido Shinkansen (Tokyo - Kyoto - Osaka)

The Tokaido Shinkansen is the oldest and busiest Shinkansen line in Japan, connecting Tokyo (Tokyo Station) to Kyoto and further to Osaka. Nozomi, Hikari, and Kodama are the types of trains running on this line, with Nozomi being the fastest, making limited stops between the two cities.

Sanyo Shinkansen (Osaka - Kyoto - Hiroshima)

The Sanyo Shinkansen connects Osaka (Shin-Osaka Station) to Kyoto and continues further to Hiroshima. This line offers trains like Nozomi and Hikari, providing efficient connections between these major cities.

Tokaido-Sanyo Shinkansen (Tokyo - Kyoto - Osaka - Hiroshima)

The combined Tokaido-Sanyo Shinkansen line links Tokyo to Kyoto, Osaka, and Hiroshima. It allows travelers to make a seamless journey from Tokyo in the east to Hiroshima in the west.

Kyushu Shinkansen (Osaka - Kyoto - Hakata)

The Kyushu Shinkansen connects Osaka (Shin-Osaka Station) to Fukuoka (Hakata Station) on the island of Kyushu, passing through Kyoto. It is a convenient option for travelers who want to explore the southwestern region of Japan.

TRADITIONAL JAPANESE ARTS

Kyoto is a city deeply rooted in traditional Japanese arts and craftsmanship. Here are some traditional Japanese arts you can experience in Kyoto:

Ikebana (Flower Arrangement)

Ikebana is the Japanese art of flower arrangement. It emphasizes simplicity, asymmetry, and the use of natural materials. Several ikebana schools in Kyoto offer workshops and demonstrations where you can learn about the principles and techniques of this elegant art form.

Calligraphy

Shodo, the art of Japanese calligraphy, is a practice of writing kanji characters using a brush and ink. In Kyoto, you can find calligraphy workshops where you can learn the basic strokes and create your own unique piece of calligraphy.

Traditional Crafts

Kyoto is renowned for its traditional crafts, each with its own long-standing history. Some of the notable crafts include:

Kyoto Pottery (Kyo-yaki/Kiyomizu-yaki)

Kyoto is famous for its pottery, known as Kyo-yaki or Kiyomizu-yaki. It encompasses a wide range of ceramic works, including tea utensils, vases, plates, and decorative pieces. The Kiyomizu-yaki district near Kiyomizu-dera Temple is a popular area to explore pottery studios and shops, where you can witness artisans at work and purchase unique ceramics.

Kimono Dressing

Kyoto is an ideal place to experience the art of kimono dressing. Many shops and studios offer kimono rental services, where you can choose from a wide variety of beautiful kimono designs and have professionals assist you in wearing them properly. Walking through the streets of Kyoto in a kimono is a delightful way to immerse yourself in Japanese culture.

Nishijin-ori (Nishijin Textiles)

Nishijin-ori is a traditional weaving technique used to produce exquisite textiles, including kimono fabric, obi (sash), and other accessories. The Nishijin district in Kyoto is known for its historic weaving houses and workshops. You can visit these establishments to observe the intricate weaving process and purchase finely crafted textiles.

Kyoto Bamboo Crafts

Bamboo crafts have a long history in Kyoto and are used to create a variety of products, such as baskets, tea utensils, and decorative items. The Arashiyama district is a hub for bamboo crafts, and visitors can explore bamboo groves, visit workshops, and even try their hand at bamboo craft-making workshops.

Lacquerware (Urushi)

Kyoto is known for its lacquerware, known as "Kyo-nuri." Lacquerware items, such as bowls, trays, and boxes, are meticulously crafted and finished with layers of urushi lacquer. The Kiyomizu-yaki district and the Higashiyama area are excellent places to find lacquerware workshops and stores where you can admire the craftsmanship and purchase unique pieces.

Kyo-yuzen (Yuzen Silk Dyeing)

Kyo-yuzen is a traditional silk dyeing technique that produces intricate and vibrant designs on kimono fabric. The designs often feature nature motifs and are hand-painted or stencil-dyed onto the fabric. Kyoto has several yuzen studios where you can witness the dyeing process and purchase beautiful yuzen textiles or accessories.

Japanese Paper (Washi)

Kyoto is known for its production of traditional Japanese paper, called "washi." Washi is made from the fibers of mulberry trees and is used for various purposes, including calligraphy, origami, and decorative art. You can visit paper-making workshops, such as the Kamisoe Paper Studio, to learn about the traditional paper-making process and purchase unique washi products.

FESTIVALS AND CELEBRATIONS

Kyoto is a city that celebrates its cultural heritage with numerous festivals and celebrations throughout the year. These events showcase traditional customs, performances, and vibrant displays. Here are some notable festivals and celebrations in Kyoto:

Gion Matsuri

Gion Matsuri, also known as the Gion Festival, is one of Japan's most famous and grandest festivals, held annually in Kyoto during the entire month of July. It is a celebration of the Gion district's rich history, culture, and religious heritage. The festival has a history that dates back over a thousand years and is considered one of Kyoto's Three Major Festivals, along with the Aoi Matsuri and the Jidai Matsuri. Here are some key highlights and traditions associated with the Gion Matsuri:

Yamaboko Floats

The main feature of the festival is the massive wooden floats known as "yamaboko." These elaborately decorated floats are constructed without the use of nails and require skilled craftsmanship. There are two types of floats: the larger "naginata-yama" with tall, elegant structures, and the smaller "yama" with compact, more intricate designs.

Yoiyama

Leading up to the main procession, the festival kicks off with "Yoiyama" evenings on July 14th and 15th. During Yoiyama, the streets in the Gion district are closed to vehicular traffic, and thousands of lanterns illuminate the area. Locals and visitors enjoy lively street stalls, performances, and festive activities.

The Procession

On July 17th, the main procession known as "Yamaboko Junko" takes place. It involves the elaborate and careful transportation of the yamaboko floats through the streets of Kyoto. The floats are pulled by teams of local men and accompanied by traditional music and performances.

Nagoshi Harai

On July 24th, the festival concludes with "Nagoshi Harai," a purification ceremony at Yasaka Shrine. People walk through a large ring made of grass to purify themselves and ward off evil spirits.

Religious Significance

Gion Matsuri has its origins in the ninth century as a religious ceremony to appease the deity and protect the city from epidemics, natural disasters, and other calamities. Over time, it evolved into a grand festival celebrating Kyoto's culture and traditions.

Saki Matsuri

Gion Matsuri actually consists of two parts: the Saki Matsuri (pre-festival) and Ato Matsuri (post-festival). The Saki Matsuri takes place from July 1st to July 5th and includes various religious rituals and events.

Gion Bayashi Music

The festival is accompanied by traditional Gion Bayashi music, played on traditional instruments like flutes, drums, and bells, creating a festive and vibrant atmosphere.

Aoi Matsuri

The Aoi Matsuri, also known as the Hollyhock Festival, is one of Kyoto's three major festivals, along with the Gion Matsuri and the Jidai Matsuri. It is a traditional event that dates back over a thousand years and takes place annually on May 15th in Kyoto, Japan. The Aoi Matsuri is a celebration of Kyoto's cultural heritage and history and is characterized by its elegant and refined atmosphere. Here are some key features and traditions associated with the Aoi Matsuri:

Costumes and Procession

The main attraction of the Aoi Matsuri is the grand procession that moves through the streets of Kyoto. The procession includes participants dressed in Heian-era court costumes, replicating the style of the imperial court during the Heian period (794-1185). The procession is led by a woman portraying Saio-Dai, who is chosen from among Kyoto's unmarried women to represent the imperial princess of the Heian court.

Hollyhock Leaves (Aoi)

The festival is named after the hollyhock leaves (aoi) used as a symbol in the event. Participants wear hollyhock leaf decorations, and the Saio-Dai carries a large hollyhock leaf bouquet as part of her attire. Hollyhocks are believed to have protective qualities and are used to purify and bless the festival.

Shimogamo Shrine and Kamigamo Shrine

The Aoi Matsuri begins at the Kyoto Imperial Palace and proceeds to the Shimogamo Shrine and then to the Kamigamo Shrine. Both shrines are important Shinto sanctuaries and serve as the main venues for various rituals and ceremonies during the festival.

Purification and Blessing

The Aoi Matsuri has its roots in ancient purification rituals aimed at warding off natural disasters and ensuring a good harvest. Today, the festival maintains its traditional essence with blessings for the well-being and prosperity of Kyoto and its people.

Participation and Community Involvement

The Aoi Matsuri involves the participation of various community organizations and local residents. It is considered a significant event that strengthens the sense of community and cultural identity in Kyoto.

Traditional Music and Dance

The procession is accompanied by traditional court music and dance, adding to the dignified and elegant ambiance of the event.

Historical Reenactment

The Aoi Matsuri serves as a historical reenactment of the grand ceremonies and processions that took place during the Heian period, allowing both locals and visitors to experience Kyoto's rich past.

Jidai Matsuri

The Jidai Matsuri, also known as the Festival of the Ages, is one of Kyoto's three major festivals, alongside the Gion Matsuri and the Aoi Matsuri. This annual event takes place on October 22nd, and it celebrates the rich history and cultural heritage of Kyoto, Japan. The Jidai Matsuri is a historical procession that showcases various periods of Kyoto's past, spanning from the Heian period (794-1185) to the Meiji period (1868-1912). Here are some key features and traditions associated with the Jidai Matsuri:

Historical Procession

The highlight of the Jidai Matsuri is the grand historical procession, which includes around 2,000 participants dressed in elaborate and historically accurate costumes representing different eras in Kyoto's history. The procession moves through the streets of Kyoto, starting from the Kyoto Imperial Palace and concluding at the Heian Shrine.

Court Nobles and Samurai

The procession features individuals dressed as court nobles, samurai warriors, artisans, and commoners from various historical periods. Each group represents the distinct clothing and customs of the respective era they portray.

Historical Reenactment

The Jidai Matsuri is a vivid reenactment of Kyoto's past, providing a visual journey through the city's historical development. The costumes, props, and decorations aim to accurately depict the lifestyles and fashion of each era.

Heian Shrine Dedication

The Jidai Matsuri concludes at the Heian Shrine, where a special dedication ceremony takes place. The shrine is dedicated to Emperor Kammu and Emperor Komei, who were significant figures in Kyoto's history.

Cultural Display

In addition to the procession, the Jidai Matsuri features cultural displays and performances at the Heian Shrine. Visitors can witness traditional arts, music, and dance, adding to the festival's festive atmosphere.

Community Involvement

Similar to other major festivals in Kyoto, the Jidai Matsuri involves the participation and support of local communities and organizations. It is a collaborative effort that strengthens the sense of cultural pride and identity in Kyoto.

Historical Significance

The Jidai Matsuri was first held in 1895 to commemorate the 1,100th anniversary of the foundation of Kyoto as Japan's capital. Since then, it has become a cherished and essential part of Kyoto's cultural heritage.

Tō-ji Temple Flea Market

The Tō-ji Temple Flea Market, also known as Tō-ji Kōbō-san Flea Market, is a popular monthly market held at Tō-ji Temple in Kyoto, Japan. It takes place on the 21st of each month and is one of the largest and most famous flea markets in the city. The market attracts both locals and tourists and offers a vibrant shopping experience with a wide variety of goods on sale. Here are some key features and information about the Tō-ji Temple Flea Market:

Location

Tō-ji Temple, officially known as Kyō-ō-gokoku-ji, is a UNESCO World Heritage Site and a significant Buddhist temple in Kyoto. The flea market is held on the temple grounds and surrounding areas.

History

The Tō-ji Temple Flea Market has a long history and tradition, dating back many centuries. It was originally established as a temple market to support the upkeep and maintenance of the temple grounds.

Goods on Sale

The market offers a wide range of goods, including antiques, second-hand items, vintage clothing, crafts, ceramics, books, plants, artwork, and various other treasures. It is an excellent place to find unique souvenirs, traditional Japanese items, and bargains.

Time and Duration

The market typically starts early in the morning and continues until around mid-afternoon. It is advisable to arrive early if you want to explore the market fully and find the best deals.

Crowds and Atmosphere

The Tō-ji Temple Flea Market can get quite busy, especially during peak tourist seasons. The lively atmosphere, bustling crowds, and diverse array of items for sale create a vibrant and enjoyable shopping experience.

Food Stalls

Alongside the various vendors selling goods, there are also food stalls offering a selection of delicious local snacks and street food. It's an excellent opportunity to savor some tasty treats while browsing the market.

Seasonal Variations

The market's offerings may vary depending on the season, with different items and themes becoming prominent during different times of the year.

Entrance Fee

There is usually no entrance fee to access the flea market area. However, some vendors may charge a fee for specific attractions or activities they offer.

Hanatoro (March and December)

Hanatoro, meaning "path of flowers and light," is an event that illuminates several historic areas of Kyoto. In March, the illuminated path stretches from Maruyama Park to Yasaka Shrine, while in December, it illuminates the Arashiyama district. Visitors can enjoy the magical ambiance created by the beautifully lit streets and temples.

Daimonji Gozan Okuribi (August)

On the evening of August 16th, Kyoto celebrates the Daimonji Gozan Okuribi, also known as the Mountain Bonfires. Large bonfires shaped like kanji characters and symbols are lit on mountains surrounding the city, symbolizing the sending off of ancestral spirits during the Obon festival.

Kyoto International Film Festival

Kyoto International Film Festival (KIFF) is an annual film festival held in Kyoto, Japan. It is a prominent event that celebrates both domestic and international films, providing a platform for filmmakers and cinephiles to come together and showcase their works. Here are some key features and aspects of the Kyoto International Film Festival:

Venue and Schedule

The festival takes place in various venues throughout Kyoto, showcasing a diverse selection of films. The event typically spans several days, during which attendees can enjoy screenings, premieres, panel discussions, workshops, and other film-related activities.

International and Domestic Films

KIFF features a wide range of films from around the world, including feature films, short films, documentaries, and animated works. It serves as a platform for filmmakers from different cultures to connect and share their stories with a global audience.

Focus on Japanese Cinema

KIFF also places a strong emphasis on promoting Japanese cinema. It provides a platform for Japanese filmmakers to present their latest creations and contributes to the recognition and appreciation of Japanese cinema both domestically and internationally.

Red Carpet Events

The festival includes glamorous red carpet events and premieres, attracting celebrities, filmmakers, and media attention. These events add a touch of glamour and excitement to the festival experience.

Awards and Recognition

KIFF awards several prizes to outstanding films and filmmakers. These awards may include Best Film, Best Director, Best Actor, Best Actress, and more. The recognition from the festival can significantly boost a film's reputation and exposure in the industry.

Cultural Exchange

In addition to showcasing films, the Kyoto International Film Festival also promotes cultural exchange by hosting events that celebrate traditional Japanese arts, music, and performances.

Community Engagement

The festival actively engages with the local community, offering screenings in various locations throughout Kyoto and involving the public in film-related activities.

DAY TRIPS FROM KYOTO

Kyoto's central location in the Kansai region of Japan makes it an ideal base for day trips to nearby cities and attractions. Here are some popular day trip destinations from Kyoto:

Nara (Approximately 45 minutes by train)

Nara is famous for its ancient temples, lush parks, and, most notably, the Nara Park where friendly wild deer roam freely. Visit Todai-ji Temple, home to the giant bronze Buddha statue, and explore the serene gardens of Isuien and Yoshikien.

Osaka (Approximately 30 minutes by train)

Osaka is a bustling metropolis known for its vibrant street food, modern architecture, and lively entertainment districts. Explore the historic Osaka Castle, stroll along the vibrant Dotonbori area, and enjoy panoramic city views from the Umeda Sky Building.

Himeji (Approximately 1 hour by train)

Himeji is home to Himeji Castle, one of Japan's most iconic and well-preserved castles. Explore the castle's impressive architecture, beautiful gardens, and panoramic views from the top. Don't miss the nearby Kokoen Garden and the Engyo-ji Temple.

Kobe (Approximately 30 minutes by train)

Located on the coast, Kobe is known for its scenic views, delicious Kobe beef, and the vibrant Chinatown district. Take a stroll along the waterfront area of Kobe Harborland, visit the Nunobiki Herb Garden and enjoy a panoramic view of the city from the Kobe Port Tower.

Arashiyama (Approximately 20 minutes by train)

Arashiyama is a picturesque district located on the western outskirts of Kyoto. Visit the famous bamboo grove, explore the beautiful gardens of Tenryu-ji Temple, and take a scenic boat ride along the Hozu River. The Monkey Park Iwatayama and the enchanting Sagano Scenic Railway are also popular attractions.

Kurama and Kibune (Approximately 30 minutes by train)

These two neighboring villages are nestled in the mountains north of Kyoto. Enjoy a peaceful hike through the lush forest to Kurama-dera Temple, soak in the healing waters of Kurama Onsen, and visit the serene Kifune Shrine, known for its magical atmosphere.

GEISHA CULTURE

Geisha culture is deeply ingrained in Kyoto's history and traditions. Geisha, known as geiko in Kyoto dialect, are highly skilled and professional entertainers who specialize in traditional Japanese arts such as dance, music, and conversation. Here's an overview of geisha culture in Kyoto:

Geisha Training

Becoming a geisha requires years of training and dedication. Young women, usually in their teenage years, enter an okiya (geisha house) to study various arts, including traditional dance, musical instruments like the shamisen, tea ceremony, and social graces. The training period can last several years before they debut as fully-fledged geisha.

Geisha Districts

Kyoto is home to several geisha districts, with the most famous being Gion and Pontocho. These areas are known for their preserved traditional architecture, narrow streets, and teahouses where geisha entertain guests. Walking through these districts provides a glimpse into the traditional ambiance and occasional sightings of geisha and maiko (apprentice geisha) adorned in elegant kimonos.

Geisha Makeup and Attire

Geisha are recognized for their distinct appearance. They wear elaborate kimonos, tied with an obi (sash), and style their hair in intricate traditional hairstyles. Geisha also apply white makeup on their face, neck, and nape, with a signature red accent on the lips. This makeup style is known as "shiro-nuri" and is an iconic part of geisha culture.

Geisha Entertainment

Geisha entertain guests with traditional performances that include dance, music, and engaging conversation. They often perform at exclusive teahouses or private parties called ozashiki, where they engage guests through games, conversation, and artistic performances. Geisha are skilled at creating a convivial atmosphere and maintaining the traditional customs of hospitality.

Maiko Apprenticeship

Maiko are young girls who undergo training to become geisha. Dressed in more vibrant and ornate kimonos, they are easily identifiable by their elaborate hairstyles and vibrant obi. Maiko entertain guests in a similar manner to geisha but are still in their training period and have distinct rituals and customs associated with their apprenticeship.

Geisha Yearly Events

Kyoto hosts several annual events related to geisha culture. Some notable events include the Miyako Odori, a traditional dance performance by geisha and maiko held in April, and the Kamogawa Odori, a series of geisha performances and dances held in May.

KYOTO'S TEA CULTURE

Kyoto is known as the birthplace and heart of Japanese tea culture. The city has a rich history and deep connection to tea, particularly in the form of matcha (powdered green tea) and the traditional Japanese tea ceremony. Here's an overview of Kyoto's tea culture:

Japanese Tea Ceremony

Kyoto is an ideal place to experience the art of the Japanese tea ceremony, also known as "chanoyu" or "sado." The tea ceremony is a highly ritualized practice that emphasizes the aesthetics, mindfulness, and hospitality associated with serving and receiving matcha. Several teahouses, tea rooms, and cultural centers in Kyoto offer opportunities to observe or partake in tea ceremonies conducted by knowledgeable tea masters.

Uji Tea

Uji, a city located near Kyoto, is famous for producing some of the highest quality tea in Japan. Uji tea, particularly matcha, is highly regarded for its rich flavor, vibrant green color, and smooth texture. Many tea houses and specialty shops in Kyoto offer Uji tea for purchase, allowing visitors to savor the distinct taste of this regional specialty.

Tea Houses and Tea Gardens

Kyoto is dotted with traditional tea houses and tea gardens where visitors can enjoy the serene and tranquil atmosphere while sipping a cup of tea. Places like the Katsura Imperial Villa, Taizo-in Temple, and the Kodai-ji Temple offer opportunities to experience tea in a traditional setting surrounded by beautiful gardens and historic architecture.

Tea Events and Festivals

Kyoto hosts various tea-related events and festivals throughout the year. One such event is the Kyoto International Tea Fair, which showcases a wide range of teas from different regions and provides opportunities for tasting and purchasing. Additionally, during the Higashiyama Hanatoro event in March, tea houses along the historic streets of Kyoto's Higashiyama district open their doors to visitors, offering a unique opportunity to enjoy tea while admiring the illuminated cherry blossoms.

Tea Ware

Kyoto is known for its production of high-quality tea ware, including tea bowls (chawan), tea caddies (cha-ire), and tea whisks (chasen). The city is home to many skilled artisans who create these traditional tea utensils using traditional techniques. Visitors can explore local pottery districts like Kiyomizu-yaki or purchase tea ware from specialty shops in Kyoto.

Tea Tourism

Kyoto offers tea enthusiasts the chance to engage in tea-related tourism experiences. Visitors can participate in hands-on activities such as tea leaf picking, tea processing workshops, and tea farm visits in Uji or other nearby tea-producing regions.

KYOTO AT NIGHT

Kyoto at night is a captivating and enchanting experience. As one of Japan's most historically and culturally significant cities, Kyoto transforms into a magical and atmospheric place after the sun sets.

Illuminated Temples and Shrines

The illuminated temples and shrines of Kyoto are a true spectacle, offering a magical experience that highlights the architectural beauty and cultural significance of these historical sites. Here are some of the most prominent temples and shrines in Kyoto that are particularly enchanting when illuminated at night:

Kiyomizu-dera

Kiyomizu-dera, also known as the Pure Water Temple, is one of Kyoto's most iconic and popular temples. When illuminated at night, the main hall and the wooden stage overlooking the city are beautifully lit, creating a breathtaking view. The temple's elevated location provides a stunning panorama of Kyoto's city lights in the background.

Fushimi Inari Taisha

Famous for its thousands of vermillion torii gates that form a winding path up the mountain, Fushimi Inari Taisha takes on an entirely different charm at night. The lanterns lining the paths and the illuminated torii gates create an otherworldly atmosphere as you explore the sacred trails.

Kinkaku-ji (The Golden Pavilion)

Kinkaku-ji, a Zen Buddhist temple covered in gold leaf, is an impressive sight during the day, but it becomes even more enchanting at night. When the golden facade is illuminated, it reflects beautifully on the calm waters of the pond, making it a postcard-worthy scene.

Ginkaku-ji (The Silver Pavilion)

While Ginkaku-ji isn't covered in silver as its name suggests, this Zen temple is a serene and elegant structure surrounded by beautiful gardens. Its understated beauty is further accentuated at night when the soft lights enhance its simple yet refined aesthetics.

Yasaka Pagoda

Located in the Higashiyama District, the Yasaka Pagoda is part of the Hokan-ji Temple and stands tall, providing a striking silhouette against the night sky. When illuminated, it offers a stunning visual in the traditional surroundings of the Gion district.

To-ji

To-ji is a significant temple in Kyoto known for its five-story pagoda, which is the tallest wooden tower in Japan. Illuminated at night, the pagoda and the temple buildings create a serene and majestic ambiance.

Eikan-do Zenrin-ji

Eikan-do Zenrin-ji is especially famous for its autumn foliage, but it's equally captivating at night. The temple's beautiful gardens and ponds, along with the illuminated maple trees, make it a serene place to visit after sunset.

Gion District

The Gion District is one of Kyoto's most iconic and historically significant areas. Known for its traditional architecture, charming streets, and association with geisha culture, Gion offers visitors a glimpse into Japan's rich cultural heritage. Here's a closer look at what makes Gion so special:

Geisha and Maiko Culture

Gion is famous for being a traditional geisha district, where geisha (geiko in the local dialect) and maiko (apprentice geisha) entertain guests with traditional music, dance, and conversation. While the number of geisha has diminished over the years, you can still spot them in their elegant kimono and distinctive hairstyles, especially in the evenings as they move between appointments.

Traditional Architecture

Gion retains much of its historical charm through its traditional wooden machiya townhouses, some of which date back to the Edo period (1603-1868). Walking through the narrow streets and alleys of Gion is like stepping back in time, providing a glimpse of what Kyoto looked like centuries ago.

Hanamikoji Street

Hanamikoji is the main street running through Gion and is a popular destination for visitors. The street is lined with teahouses, restaurants, and shops. In the evening, the lanterns hanging outside the establishments create a magical ambiance, and it's not uncommon to spot geisha and maiko gracefully making their way to appointments.

Gion Corner

Gion Corner is a cultural center where visitors can experience traditional arts and performances, including tea ceremonies, ikebana (flower arranging), gagaku (court music), and geisha dance. It's an excellent opportunity to get a taste of Kyoto's traditional arts in one place.

Kobu Kaburenjo Theater

This theater in Gion is where you can watch authentic maiko dance performances. The graceful movements and colorful attire of the maiko and geisha create an unforgettable experience.

Shirakawa Canal

The Shirakawa Canal is a picturesque waterway that runs through Gion. The charming scene of traditional teahouses and restaurants lining the canal, along with the weeping willow trees, is particularly enchanting during cherry blossom season and in the evening when the area is illuminated.

Yasaka Shrine

While not located directly within the Gion District, Yasaka Shrine is within walking distance and is a significant Shinto shrine in Kyoto. It hosts various festivals and events throughout the year, making it a lively and cultural hub for visitors.

Pontocho Alley

Pontocho Alley is a narrow, atmospheric alley located in the heart of Kyoto, running parallel to the Kamogawa River. It is one of the city's most charming and historic areas, known for its traditional architecture, lantern-lit streets, and a wide variety of dining and entertainment options. Here's what makes Pontocho Alley a popular destination for both locals and visitors:

Traditional Architecture

Pontocho Alley is lined with traditional wooden machiya buildings that exude a nostalgic and old-world charm. Many of these buildings house restaurants, teahouses, bars, and shops, retaining the architectural character of old Kyoto.

Lantern-Lit Ambiance

As night falls, Pontocho Alley comes alive with the soft glow of lanterns illuminating the street. The warm and intimate lighting adds to the romantic and historical atmosphere, making it a perfect place for a leisurely evening stroll.

Dining and Izakayas

Pontocho is well-known for its array of restaurants and izakayas (Japanese-style pubs). These establishments serve a diverse range of Japanese cuisine, from traditional Kyoto dishes to modern interpretations. Many of them offer outdoor seating along the riverbank, providing a picturesque setting for dining.

Kamogawa River Views

The alley's proximity to the Kamogawa River allows visitors to enjoy pleasant views of the water while dining or walking. During the warmer months, people often sit along the riverbanks and enjoy the fresh air and scenic beauty.

Geisha Sightings

While Gion is the more famous geisha district in Kyoto, it's not uncommon to spot geisha or maiko walking along Pontocho Alley, especially during evenings. Seeing these elegantly dressed women adds to the allure of the area.

Noryo Yuka

In the summer, some restaurants set up noryo yuka, temporary wooden platforms extending over the river, where patrons can dine while enjoying the cool breeze and beautiful river views.

Cultural Events

Pontocho Alley occasionally hosts traditional events, such as seasonal festivals and performances, providing visitors with an opportunity to experience Japanese culture up close.

Late-Night Atmosphere

Pontocho's narrow and dimly lit alleys create an intimate and mysterious ambiance, making it an excellent spot for a late-night stroll or a drink after dinner.

Kamo River

The Kamo River (Kamo-gawa) is a picturesque waterway that flows through the heart of Kyoto, Japan. It is one of the most iconic and beloved natural features of the city, offering both locals and visitors a tranquil escape from the urban bustle. Here are some key features and attractions related to the Kamo River:

Scenic Beauty

The Kamo River is known for its scenic beauty, especially during the cherry blossom season in spring and the changing foliage in autumn. The riverbanks are adorned with cherry trees and maple trees, creating a stunning landscape that attracts numerous visitors for hanami (flower viewing) picnics and leisurely walks.

Leisure Activities

The riverbanks provide a serene setting for various leisure activities. Locals and tourists alike enjoy picnicking, jogging, cycling, or simply relaxing on the grassy riverbanks. The riverside is a popular spot for both individuals and families to spend quality time outdoors.

Kamogawa Delta

Towards the eastern end of the river, the Kamo River splits into two branches, forming the Kamogawa Delta. The delta area features small islands and several bridges, adding to the charm of the riverscape.

Sanjo Bridge and Shijo Bridge

Two of the most famous bridges that cross the Kamo River are the Sanjo Bridge and Shijo Bridge. These bridges are important landmarks and offer great views of the river and surrounding scenery.

Summer Festivals

During the summer, the Kamo River is a central part of the traditional Gozan no Okuribi (Daimonji) festival, where large bonfires in the shape of Japanese characters are lit on the nearby mountainsides, and the reflection can be seen on the river's surface.

Dining by the River

Many restaurants and cafes with outdoor seating are located along the riverbanks, providing an excellent opportunity to enjoy a meal or a drink while admiring the scenic views.

Firefly Watching

In early summer, firefly viewing events are sometimes organized along the Kamo River. This magical experience allows visitors to see these bioluminescent insects lighting up the riverbanks.

Walking and Cycling Path

A pedestrian and bicycle path runs along the river's edge, making it easy to explore the area on foot or by bike.

Nightlife and Entertainment

Kyoto's nightlife and entertainment scene offer a mix of traditional and modern experiences, catering to various interests and preferences. While it may not be as vibrant as the nightlife in Tokyo, Kyoto still has plenty to offer after the sun sets. Here are some of the popular nightlife and entertainment options in Kyoto:

Pontocho Alley

Pontocho Alley comes alive at night with its lantern-lit ambiance and a wide array of restaurants, teahouses, and bars. It's an excellent place to enjoy a traditional Kyoto dining experience or simply take a leisurely stroll along the river.

Gion Corner

For a taste of Kyoto's traditional arts, head to Gion Corner. This cultural center offers a showcase of traditional performances, including tea ceremonies, flower arranging, traditional music, and dance.

Izakayas and Bars

Kyoto has a variety of izakayas and bars where you can enjoy casual dining, drinks, and socializing. These places often offer a lively atmosphere and a chance to try local sake and other Japanese beverages.

Kiyamachi Street

Parallel to the Kamo River, Kiyamachi Street is another popular nightlife area in Kyoto. It features a range of restaurants, bars, and clubs, making it a go-to spot for those seeking a more modern and bustling nightlife experience.

Karaoke

Karaoke is a popular entertainment option in Japan, and Kyoto has several karaoke venues where you can sing your heart out in private rooms with friends or family.

Nishiki Market at Night

Nishiki Market, Kyoto's famous food market, offers a unique experience in the evening. Some shops and eateries stay open after dark, serving delicious street food and local specialties.

Gion Odori

If you visit Kyoto during November, you can enjoy the Gion Odori, a traditional dance performance held by geisha and maiko in the Gion district. It's a fantastic opportunity to witness traditional arts and culture.

Night Cruises

Several companies offer boat cruises along the Kamo River, providing a different perspective of the city's landmarks beautifully lit up at night.

Clubbing and Music Events

While Kyoto's club scene may not be as extensive as in larger cities, you can still find clubs and music events featuring both local and international DJs and bands.

Izakayas and Local Cuisine

Izakayas and local cuisine are an integral part of the dining experience in Kyoto. Izakayas are traditional Japanese pubs that offer a casual and social setting for eating, drinking, and socializing with friends, family, or colleagues. They serve a variety of small dishes, making it easy to try different flavors and specialties. When in Kyoto, here are some local dishes and izakayas you should consider trying:

Kaiseki Cuisine

Kyoto is famous for kaiseki, a multi-course traditional Japanese meal that highlights seasonal and local ingredients. Kaiseki typically consists of beautifully presented dishes, showcasing the chef's creativity and skill. Many high-end restaurants in Kyoto offer kaiseki meals, and they are a fantastic way to experience the city's culinary artistry.

Yudofu

Yudofu is a simple yet delicious Kyoto specialty made with soft tofu simmered in a savory kombu (seaweed) and soy sauce broth. It is a popular dish, especially during the colder months, and can be found in various restaurants and izakayas around the city.

Obanzai

Obanzai refers to Kyoto-style home-cooked dishes, usually made with locally sourced and seasonal ingredients. Many izakayas in Kyoto serve obanzai dishes, offering an authentic taste of the region's culinary heritage.

Sushi and Sashimi

While Kyoto is not traditionally known for its sushi like coastal cities, you can still find excellent sushi and sashimi restaurants in the city, including some izakayas that offer fresh and delicious seafood options.

Nabe (Hot Pot)

Nabe is a popular winter dish in Japan, and Kyoto's version often includes local vegetables and tofu simmered in a flavorful broth. Many izakayas serve nabe dishes, allowing you to share a hot pot with friends or family.

Yakitori

Yakitori, grilled skewered chicken, is a favorite izakaya dish. In Kyoto, you can find yakitori made from free-range local chickens, offering a unique and tasty experience.

Sake and Local Beverages

Kyoto is home to many sake breweries, and you should not miss the opportunity to try some local sake. Many izakayas offer a wide selection of sake, allowing you to explore different varieties and flavors.

Okonomiyaki

Although not a traditional Kyoto dish, you can find okonomiyaki restaurants in the city. Okonomiyaki is a savory pancake made with various ingredients like cabbage, meat, seafood, and topped with a special sauce.

Arashiyama at Night

Arashiyama, a picturesque district located on the western outskirts of Kyoto, is well-known for its natural beauty, historical landmarks, and serene atmosphere. While it is a popular destination during the day, Arashiyama at night offers a different and equally enchanting experience. Here's what you can expect when visiting Arashiyama after dark:

Illuminated Bamboo Grove

The Bamboo Grove is one of Arashiyama's main attractions, and during the day, it can get quite crowded. However, at night, the grove takes on a serene and mystical ambiance as it is softly illuminated with strategically placed lights. The tall bamboo stalks create an ethereal atmosphere, making it an ideal time for a peaceful and romantic stroll.

Togetsukyo Bridge

Togetsukyo Bridge, which spans across the Katsura River, offers stunning views of Arashiyama's scenic landscape. At night, the bridge is often illuminated, providing a charming setting for a leisurely walk or simply enjoying the reflections of the lights on the water.

Boat Ride on the Katsura River

While boat rides along the Katsura River are a popular daytime activity, some companies offer special evening cruises during certain seasons. A boat ride at night allows you to enjoy the tranquil beauty of the river and the illuminated surroundings.

Arashiyama Monkey Park Iwatayama

Although the monkey park itself closes in the late afternoon, you can still see the monkeys from outside their enclosure at the base of the mountain. The park's lights cast a soft glow on the area, providing a unique experience of observing the monkeys at night.

Nighttime Dining

Arashiyama offers various restaurants and teahouses that stay open in the evening. You can savor traditional Kyoto dishes and enjoy the local cuisine in a more relaxed and less crowded setting.

Kimono Forest

The Kimono Forest, located near the Randen Arashiyama Station, features a collection of cylindrical pillars decorated with colorful kimono fabric patterns. These pillars are illuminated at night, creating a captivating and artistic display.

Nighttime Events and Festivals

Depending on the time of your visit, there might be special nighttime events or festivals taking place in Arashiyama. These events often include traditional performances, light displays, or seasonal celebrations.

ITINERARIES

Kyoto Highlights (3 Days)

Day 1: Visit Kinkaku-ji (Golden Pavilion), Ryoan-ji Temple & Zen Garden, Ninnaji Temple.

Day 2: Explore Fushimi Inari Taisha, Gion District, Yasaka Shrine, and Maruyama Park.

Day 3: Visit Kiyomizu-dera Temple, Nijo Castle, and Arashiyama Bamboo Grove.

Cultural Immersion (4 Days)

Day 1: Explore Kiyomizu-dera Temple, Sannenzaka, and Ninenzaka Streets.

Day 2: Experience a tea ceremony, visit Nijo Castle, and take a kimono rental experience.

Day 3: Visit Kokedera (Moss Temple), Adashino Nenbutsu-ji Temple, and Ryoan-ji Temple.

Day 4: Enjoy Arashiyama Bamboo Grove, Tenryu-ji Temple, and Togetsukyo Bridge.

Nature & Scenic Beauty (4 Days)

Day 1: Explore the Philosopher's Path, Eikando Zenrinji Temple, and Nanzen-ji Temple.

Day 2: Visit Kibune Shrine and Kurama-dera Temple, and relax at Kurama Onsen.

Day 3: Explore Arashiyama Monkey Park Iwatayama and Okochi Sanso Villa.

Day 4: Discover Sagano Bamboo Forest, Tenryu-ji Temple, and Togetsukyo Bridge.

Kyoto with Kids (3 Days)

Day 1: Visit Kyoto Aquarium, Umekoji Steam Locomotive Museum, and To-ji Temple Flea Market (if on the 21st of the month).

Day 2: Explore the Kyoto Railway Museum and enjoy a boat ride on Kamo River.

Day 3: Visit the Kyoto Municipal Zoo and enjoy Maruyama Park and its playground.

Kyoto and Nara (5 Days)

Day 1: Explore Kiyomizu-dera Temple, Sannenzaka, and Ninenzaka Streets.

Day 2: Visit Fushimi Inari Taisha and Nijo Castle in Kyoto.

Day 3: Take a day trip to Nara to see Todai-ji Temple, Nara Park, and Kasuga Taisha.

Day 4: Visit Kinkaku-ji (Golden Pavilion) and Ryoan-ji Temple in Kyoto.

Day 5: Explore Arashiyama Bamboo Grove and Tenryu-ji Temple.

Gourmet Experience (3 Days)

Day 1: Savor Kyoto's culinary delights in Nishiki Market and Pontocho Alley.

Day 2: Try traditional kaiseki at a ryokan and visit Gion District for upscale dining.

Day 3: Enjoy Kyoto's local cuisine in the local izakayas and experience yuba (tofu skin) dishes.

Kyoto Festivals (2 Days)

Day 1: Explore Gion and Pontocho, and if during Gion Matsuri (July), join the festivities.

Day 2: Experience Arashiyama Onsen and enjoy the To-ji Temple Flea Market (if on the 21st of the month).

MAPS

Japan Map

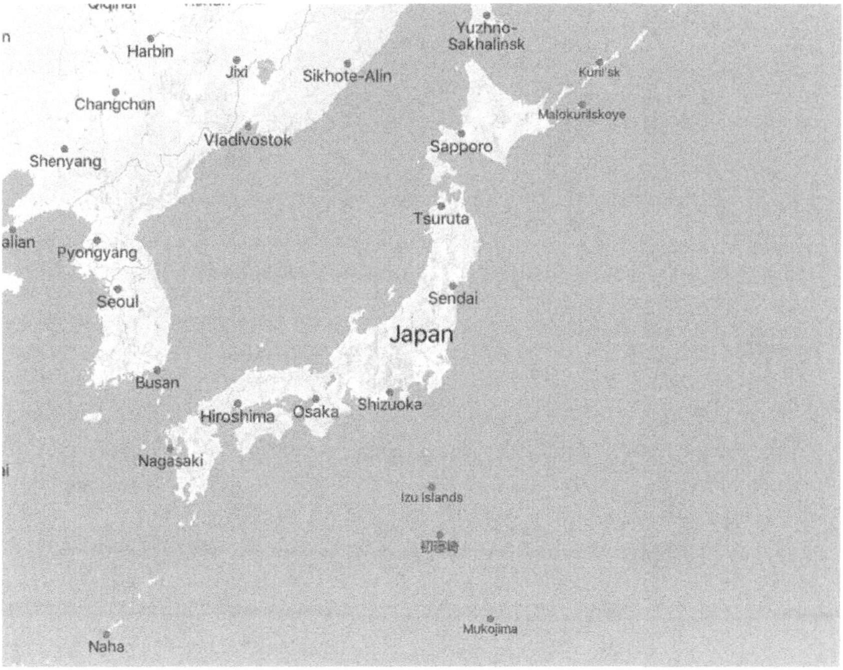

Kyoto Map

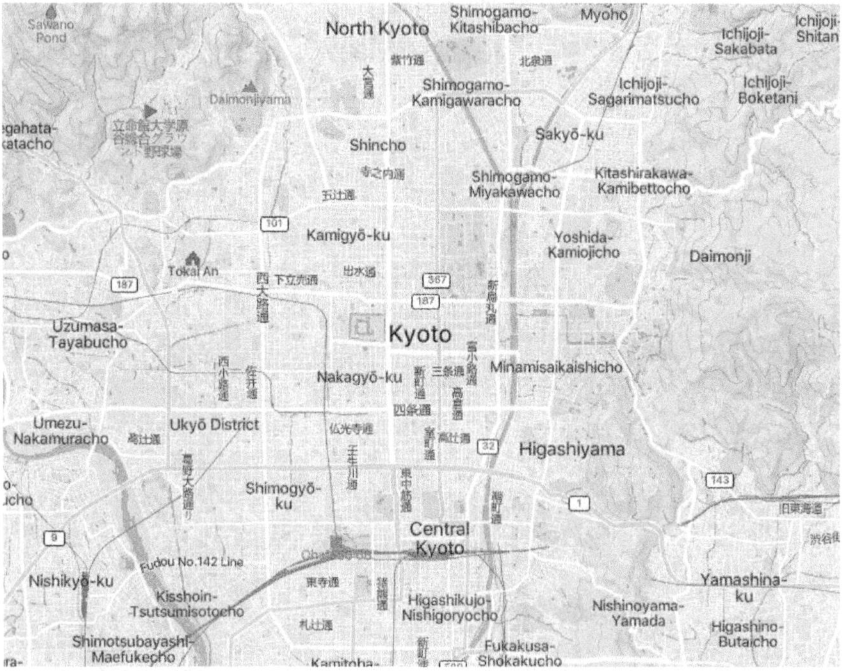
North Kyoto
Shimogamo-
Kitashibacho
Myoho
Ichijoji-
Sakabata
Daimonjiyama
Shimogamo-
Kamigawaracho
Ichijoji-
Sagarimatsucho
Ichijoji-
Boketani
Sakyō-ku
Shincho
Shimogamo-
Miyakawacho
Kitashirakawa-
Kamibettocho
101
Kamigyō-ku
Yoshida-
Kamiojicho
Daimonji
Tokai An
187
367
187
Uzumasa-
Tayabucho
Kyoto
Nakagyō-ku
Minamisaikaishicho
Umezu-
Nakamuracho
Ukyō District
32
Higashiyama
143
Shimogyō-
ku
1
9
Central
Kyoto
Fudou No.142 Line
Nishikyō-ku
Kisshoin-
Tsutsumisotocho
Higashikujo-
Nishigoryocho
Nishinoyama-
Yamada
Yamashina-
ku
Higashino-
Butaicho
Shimotsubayashi-
Maefukecho
Fukakusa-
Shokakucho

Kyoto Restaurants Map

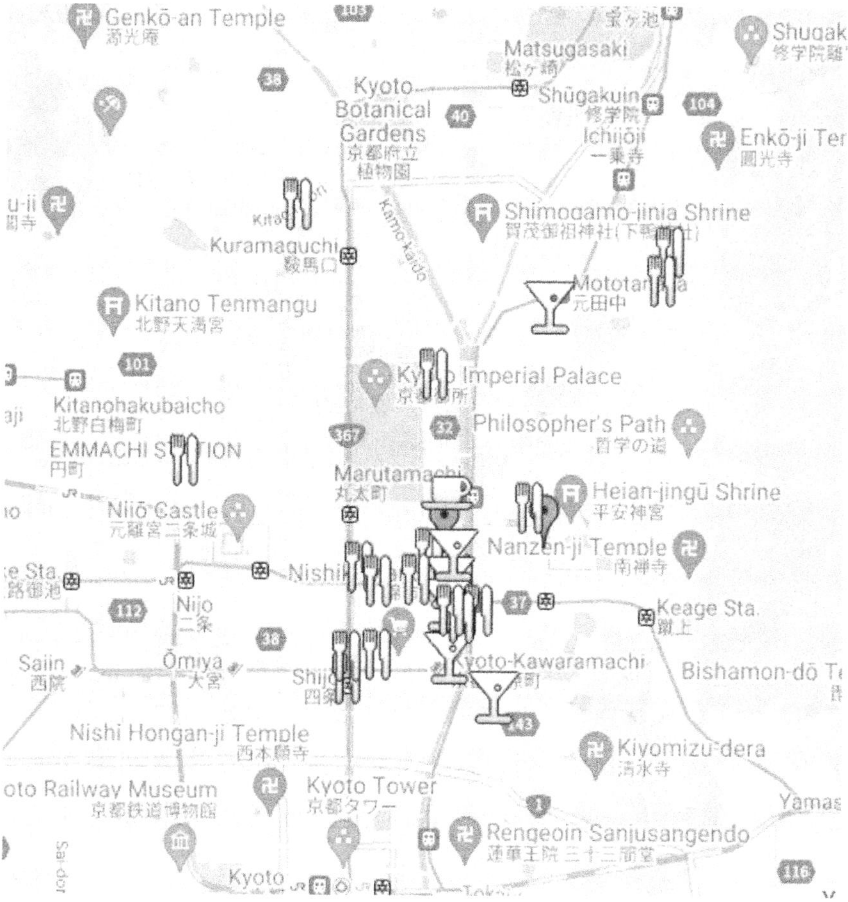

Kyoto Shrines & Temples Map

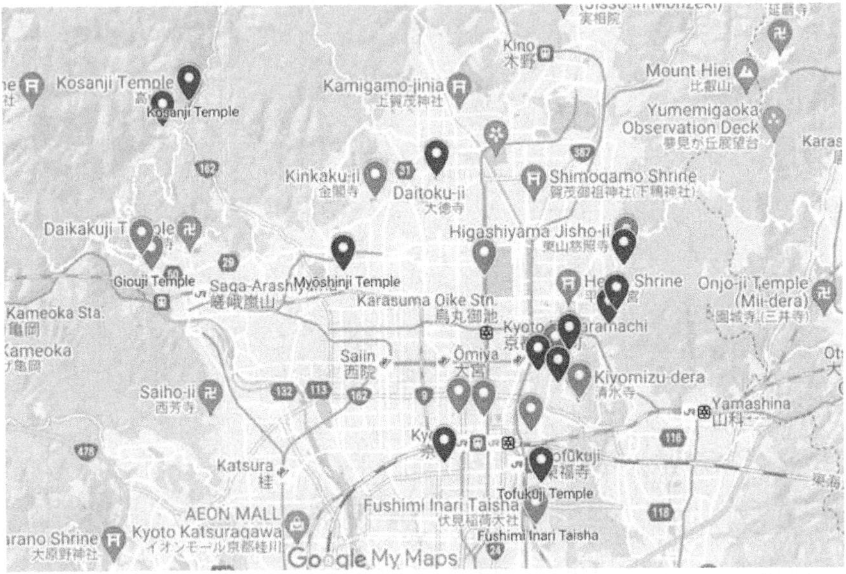

Kyoto cherry blossom map

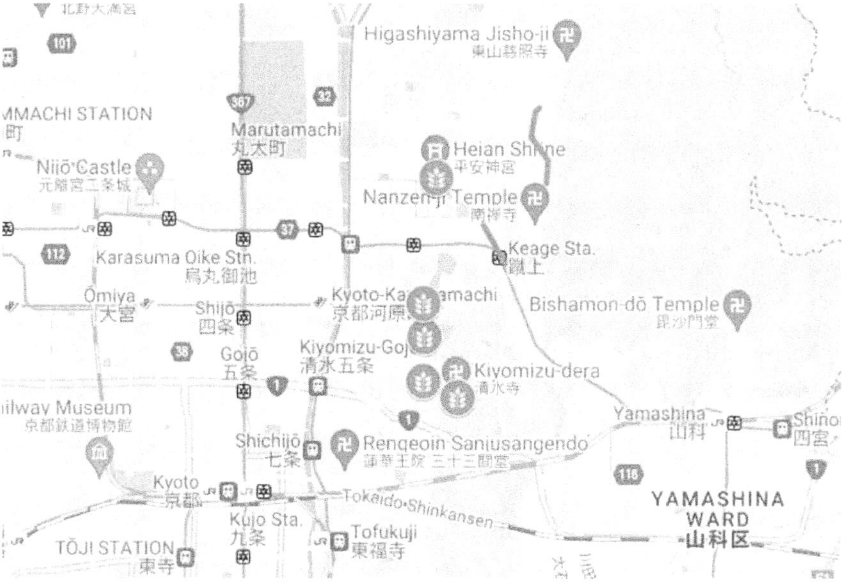

Historic Monuments of Ancient Kyoto

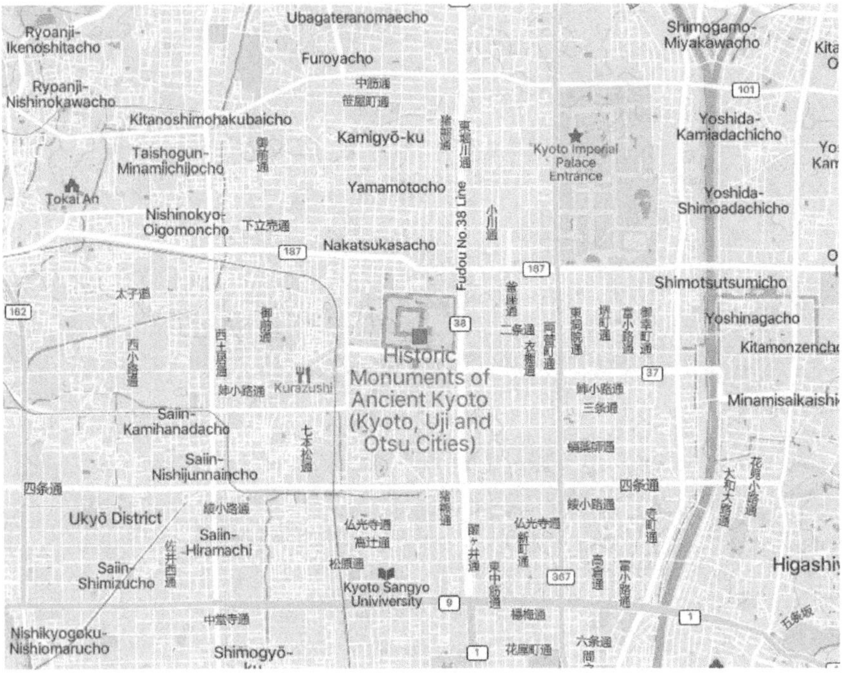

CONCLUSION

As we conclude our journey through Kyoto's timeless beauty, we hope you have been captivated by the city's rich cultural heritage, breathtaking temples, Zen gardens, and traditional arts. Kyoto's ability to preserve its ancient traditions while embracing the modern world is truly remarkable.

In this city, time seems to slow down, allowing visitors to immerse themselves in the tranquil ambiance and connect with the essence of Japan's past. Whether you are an art enthusiast, a spiritual seeker, or a nature lover, Kyoto offers a profound and transformative experience.

Beyond 2023, Kyoto will continue to evolve and adapt, embracing new technologies and innovations while staying true to its roots. The city's enduring allure lies in its ability to retain its timeless beauty, making it a destination that will continue to inspire and captivate visitors for generations to come.

So, pack your bags, embark on this extraordinary journey, and allow Kyoto to unfold its magic before you. Immerse yourself in the serenity of its temples, find solace in the harmony of its Zen gardens, and witness the enduring legacy of traditional Japanese arts. Kyoto awaits, ready to enchant and amaze you with its timeless beauty.

INDEX

Made in the USA
Las Vegas, NV
10 February 2024

85625431R00154